The Miracles
and the Resurrection

THEOLOGICAL COLLECTIONS
3

THE MIRACLES AND THE RESURRECTION

Some Recent Studies by

I. T. Ramsey

G. H. Boobyer

F. N. Davey

M. C. Perry

Henry J. Cadbury

WIPF & STOCK · Eugene, Oregon

Wipf and Stock Publishers
199 W 8th Ave, Suite 3
Eugene, OR 97401

The Miracles and the Resurrection
By Ramsey, Ian T. and Boobyer, G. H.
Copyright©1964 SPCK
ISBN 13: 978-1-60899-728-2
Publication date 6/15/2010
Previously published by SPCK, 1964

This Edition reprinted by Wipf and Stock Publishers
by arrangement with SPCK, London.

CONTENTS

Publisher's Note   vii

1. MIRACLES: AN EXERCISE IN LOGICAL MAPWORK, by Ian T. Ramsey, Nolloth Professor of the Philosophy of the Christian Religion in the University of Oxford. *An Inaugural Lecture delivered before the University of Oxford on 7 December 1951.*   1

2. THE GOSPEL MIRACLES: VIEWS PAST AND PRESENT, by G. H. Boobyer, Head of the Department of Divinity in the University of Newcastle-upon-Tyne.   31

3. HEALING IN THE NEW TESTAMENT, by F. N. Davey.   50

4. BELIEVING THE MIRACLES AND PREACHING THE RESURRECTION, by M. C. Perry, Chief Assistant for Home Publishing, S.P.C.K.   64

5. INTIMATIONS OF IMMORTALITY IN THE THOUGHT OF JESUS, by Henry J. Cadbury, formerly Hollis Professor of Divinity, Harvard Divinity School. *The Ingersoll Lecture for 1959 at Harvard University.*   79

PUBLISHER'S NOTE

THIS VOLUME is one of a series of publications bringing together in convenient and permanent form some of the occasional work of contemporary theologians. The importance of these collections certainly does not lie in any predetermined unity. None of them has been in any sense planned as a symposium. In none of them has an editorial hand, except as regards the selection of material, played any but the most minor part. If they have importance it is rather because they reveal what professional theologians, most of them teachers or one-time teachers of theology, have had at the top of their minds when they were called upon to speak or to lecture on some given subject, or to offer an interim report of some actual preoccupation. For in nearly every case the material of these studies has been originally put together for a particular occasion, and in preparing them for publication no attempt has been made to conceal the circumstances of their composition.

Yet that they have been selected to form part of a volume does mean that they are thought to have more than occasional importance. For this reason some of them have been reprinted from periodicals in which they have already appeared. Moreover, because they are brought together as illuminating a single theme (although originally written quite independently, and although approaching that theme in quite different ways) it is hoped that they will be significant as collections; that they will show what are felt to be the pressing issues in a particular field of study. The purpose is therefore to report, to inform, and to stimulate further study; and it is hoped that they will be of interest not only to scholars and students but also to those many who for various reasons have no time for systematic study but are nevertheless interested in its progress.

The first volume in this series, *On the Authority of the Bible*, (1960) contained studies by Leonard Hodgson, C. F. Evans,

John Burnaby, Gerhard Ebeling, and D. E. Nineham dealing with various aspects of the question raised by its title. Then followed *The Communication of the Gospel in New Testament Times* (1961) by Austin Farrer, C. F. Evans, J. M. Emerton, F. W. Beare, R. A. Markus, and F. W. Dillistone. This was relevant to the same theme, because it examined the growth and expression of some key ideas of the New Testament and discussed the shape and content of the apostolic kerygma. Neither of these volumes was of merely academic interest. The Bible is the book of a living Church which is still charged with the duty of communicating the Gospel, and the past has lessons which we still need to learn to-day. Similarly with this third volume. The concept of the miraculous is a frequent stumbling-block, alike to inquirer, apologist, preacher, and congregation; yet it is so integral to the biblical presentation of the Gospel of the Risen Christ that its challenge cannot be evaded.

I

MIRACLES
An Exercise in Logical Mapwork [1]

I. T. RAMSEY

ONE of the happier results of compulsory retirement from University Chairs is that it enables a new occupant to pay tribute to at least his immediate predecessor in language that need not have epitaph extravagance. But the present case has an even more gratifying feature; the forthright honesty due to present colleagues extends happily not only to my immediate predecessor but to both my predecessors, as well to Dr Webb as to Dr Grensted. How appropriate for a Chair of Christian Philosophy that duty and pleasure, tradition and truth, should be so mixed!

This year Dr Webb "comes of age" in his retirement and, as in a second youth, continues to exercise that philosophical insight, at once critical and constructive, which for over sixty-five years has been accompanied by an historical penetration and a discerning sympathy. A not dissimilar vision and sympathy we rightly associate with Dr Grensted, whose broad interests and manifold abilities never fail to arouse our admiration, and whose unassuming friendliness somewhat conceals both the vigour and the success with which he has commended psychology to the theologians and theology to the psychologists. It is a succession into which I come with understandable pride, but I rejoice most of all in the bonds of friendship which unite me to my predecessors, as I also rejoice to belong with them to that Society of which Matthew Arnold, John Newman, and Joseph Butler were members, to that College of which

[1] An Inaugural Lecture delivered before the University of Oxford on 7 December 1951. Reprinted by permission of The Clarendon Press.

Charles Frederick Nolloth, the Founder of this Chair, was a notable son. Nor do I at this time forget another Society which nurtured me for many years and whose giants included Cudworth and Paley, Milton, Darwin, and Smuts. It is a happy thought that these landmarks in the academic countryside and beyond are so widely placed as to bring inspiration without demanding blind devotion; and we are able to have them in view, and yet to steer an individual course ourselves. Which no doubt brings us near to the theme of maps and mapwork, and so appropriately to a brief consideration of the title I have given this lecture.

To construct an ordinary map is to express schematically the geographical setting of towns and villages in terms of the symbols for hills and rivers, roads and railways. Working with this analogy we may say that logical mapwork is somewhat similarly concerned to exhibit the propositional settings in which concepts are set, to exhibit the linguistic context in which the particular concept sentences have their place. In this lecture we are to be concerned especially with the concept of miracle and we shall explicate its propositional setting as we might explain where a town was by giving its context of hills and rivers, roads and railways.

We shall not do this by examining various sorts of miracle-sentence to see wherein lie their logical peculiarities and syntactical interest, though this would be a much more usual sort of exercise in logical mapwork. Rather shall we examine the broad features of one or two language maps, so see whether a place can be found on any of them for the town of "miracle".

There are two reasons for this somewhat untypical procedure:

1. In trying to plot our town "miracle" on maps of wide range we shall hope at the same time also to outline the possibility of having *one* comprehensive language map which would link together, for example, the languages of science and history. We shall indeed hope to say something relevant, even if in outline, about the possibility of an empirical metaphysics.

2. The wider the range the less likely are we to keep apart questions of logic and questions of fact. A danger it seems to me of the more typical procedure is not so much that it overlooks the factual reference as that it suggests, if only by implication, that the factual peculiarities to which the logical peculiarities bear witness

cannot be more than a function of what are called "observable facts". The widening of our language map will make it plain not only that there is no sacrosanct class of data to be called "observable facts", but that not even all functions of such "observable facts" exhaust that of which we have awareness. Different maps display different pictures of the countryside—each language, scientific or historical, for example, displays its own brand of "facts". The countryside we live in, however, is never exhausted by any one map or any number of them. Somehow it combines and includes all the facts which each map in its own way characteristically portrays, and is more. Likewise that of which we are aware is not reducible without residue to "observable facts"—it combines and includes them, and is more. Not only must we see then the logical peculiarities of miracle-sentences (which might perhaps be described more strikingly by the alternative procedure), but we must also make it our business to see what is this curious sort of "fact" which it is the function of those logical peculiarities to commend, and this may be clearer, I say, by making our exercise in logical mapwork as broad as possible. But let us leave the matter there for now. At any rate I have put my cards on the table.

It will be clear now that there were two reasons for my particular choice of title:

1. I am hoping that the lecture will illustrate by implication something of the concerns of contemporary philosophy, something of its habits and disciplines, though, as I have said, it will present a much broader, less detailed and less colourful canvas than those which would commonly be found in linguistic studios to-day; and

2. By engaging in such an actual exercise we may perhaps see better than in any other way the sort of contribution which contemporary philosophy might make to Christian thinking.

We shall now examine the broad characteristics of the languages of natural science, of history, and of metaphysics, and ask ourselves whether a place can be found anywhere, and if so in what sort of setting, for the word "miracle".

First, then, some general remarks on the logical structure of the language of science.

A typical scientific assertion would be "Water boils at 100° C." introduced and commended in relation to a few features of a particular situation, e.g. a school laboratory; forty third-form boys;

steam rising all over the place; and most thermometers reading somewhere between (say) 99·9° and 100·1° when all personal factors like squinting and carelessness have been allowed for. In other words, science begins from a certain make-believe, and hazards the verbal recommendations it does, in relation to a few features selected from a given situation. It trusts that, in the generalization that results, all relevant features of future situations have been selected and described. It takes a risk. Here indeed—in reference to this "risk"—arises the so-called "justification of induction". For such a selection of characteristics as we have mentioned becomes, in the way we have seen, the topic of what is called, happily or not, an "inductive generalization". Now what makes such a generalization justified or not is, with regard to the particular characteristics involved, the measure of mutual relevance they have to one another, which affects the degree to which they are jointly isolatable from the wider environment in which they are set. Depending on how far this condition of "compactness" is satisfied, comes the possibility or not of extending the generalization to other situations. To ask for a justification of induction is really, then, to ask a question about the stability of a particular abstractive insight in regard to the widest possible variation of background. It is obvious that, for the most part, no justification can be any more than temporary. Hence it is that scientific progress depends first on a scientific stubbornness which for a time refuses to think that a primitive recommendation can possibly be wrong, and which refuses to believe that it has not discovered a permanently stable abstractive insight. But this stubbornness must pass at a later stage into a complete readiness to allow for modification when the abstractive insight is upset, and in scientific method this rhythm of stubbornness–readiness is repeated as often as need be.

To go back to our example: scientific stubbornness may for a time preserve the generalization about water boiling, by talking about inaccurate thermometers, dirty beakers, impure water, and so on, but language resistance eventually breaks, and when water is boiled in deep shelters or on tall mountains (the word "boil" being taken rightly or wrongly as an invariant) the original assertion is said to be incomplete, and is then expanded so as to read, for example, "Water boils at 100° C. at *normal* pressure". This new recommendation has obviously the advantage of a greater range than its predecessor, which indeed it includes and goes beyond.

The next stage in scientific language would be reached when a variety of sentences relating to boiling water at different temperatures and pressures were all united by some sort of hypothesis worked, say, in terms of atomic particles in perpetual motion. But science would not finish there. Sub-atomic phenomena, which necessitate our talking, for example, about "heavy water", would demand that at some stage the crude atomic hypothesis is *in toto* set aside and some new (say) electron hypothesis devised, with all the previous coverage and more, but at the cost of a more abstract level. In such a way as this, to take a different example, phlogiston theories, oxygen theories, and electron theories have been related in succession to the facts of combustion.

In other words, simple scientific sentences by what we may call their *expansibility* and hypotheses by their *convertibility* are all developed with one aim: towards a comprehensive language dealing with uniformities and repeated patterns. It is this desire to combine uniformity with comprehensiveness that makes stubbornness–readiness the curious but necessary feature of scientific practice that it is.

While scientific language tries for a time to exclude facts which are apparently unwilling to conform, yet it must always work towards a greater and greater inclusiveness. The result is that when at last it includes some unwilling fact into its scheme it finds, at the first move, that its success has turned to defeat in its mouth, for the unwilling fact has now modified the hypothesis which has embraced it. But on reflection it can be content: the old uniformity, and more, is in the new uniformity to which the modified hypothesis relates. An obtuse fact which for a time resists the generalizations of scientific method is rather like a cheeky little mouse which finds itself ultimately enclosed in the crafty cat's jaws. Admittedly, it has the satisfaction of reflecting that, when the cat's digestion has reckoned with its bones and body, the cat will never be the same cat again. But the cat too is content enough: it is still a cat—and the mouse (as the philosophers would say) is transcended in a larger uniformity.

After that general sketch of scientific language, it is appropriate for our purpose to ask: can such a language scheme, with the permanent possibility of growth by these features of expansibility and convertibility, ever be by itself totally adequate as a language map? Certainly it can succeed in becoming progressively more and more comprehensive as each modification is made. But must there not always be something which its language does not, and cannot express? There are indeed two permanent limitations on scientific language:

1. *Its permanent incompleteness.* No matter how many more features are correlated as the language is expanded; no matter how universal scientific techniques become, scientific language at any stage, no matter how far advanced, is always incomplete. For on the one hand the facts themselves will always be inexhaustible. Space-time will always be infinitely divisible and infinitely extensible; any causal series (even if only regular sequence) will be doubly infinite. It was, of course, in part to allow for points such as these that Kant introduced his regulative use of the Ideas of Reason to round off scientific thinking. Further, while the question "Why?" may in certain circumstances initiate science, it always leads ultimately beyond it, to what have been called the "limiting questions" of science, indicating that the language system of science can never be closed; that *scientific language* is never complete. Nor is this all.

2. *Its peculiar selectivity.* Scientific language begins only when, as a necessary part of its progress, it has deliberately ignored many features of the situation it is concerned to describe. How little indeed about the life of a school laboratory—even of a particular boiling experiment—is contained in the sentence "Water boils at 100° C." and sentences like it. But not only does scientific language make in this way a positive exclusion of certain features as the cost of its first penetration into the facts of a given situation; such greater inclusiveness as it thereafter gains is always at the cost of moving to more and more abstract levels. The gain in scientific coverage, which comes from expansibility and convertibility, seems always to be at the expense of increased abstraction—saying less and less about that part of a concrete situation with and from which a beginning was made, in order to say more and more about the concrete totality of facts over which scientific language is farther and farther extended:

↑ Language gaining in coverage, but relating to facts more and more abstractively distant from the initial concrete situation	nth selection: facts$_n$ and language$_n$ 2nd selection: facts$_2$ and language$_2$ 1st selection: facts$_1$ and language$_1$	. . . .	←"facts" initially surveyed→ . . . .

←—TOTAL CONCRETE FACT—→

In the face then of such inadequacies as we have just mentioned, scientific language could hardly claim of itself to offer total coverage in the sense of being a completely *adequate* account of all facts as they are *concretely* given. Scientific language may detail uniformities more and more comprehensively; but its very success in so doing means that its pictures are more and more outline sketches of concrete, given fact. Indeed, the various sciences—from astrophysics to physiology, from metallurgy to botany, provide us with countless pictures, and before leaving this question of scientific language we may raise one further problem, which will be relevant later. Clearly it is the ultimate hope of scientific language somehow to construct one picture—to link together the various pictures provided by the various "sciences". Hence, the most exciting and far-reaching scientific work is precisely that which is done in mixed fields, for example, to do with brain-potentials (uniting physics and physiology), or in an earlier day with the electronic theory of valency (uniting physics and chemistry). But such a wide-ranging language would still have the concreteness of its relevance compromised in the two ways we have described—and indeed the tragedy is that the very *scientific* language likely to be the *best* co-ordinator is naturally that whose factual reference is most abstract. The more scientific language finds its unity *in itself*, the more does it parody the facts it endeavours to describe. So we may reasonably suggest that *both* to unite scientific languages at their different abstractive levels *as well as* to give *all* levels their factual reference, words will be wanted which lie outside all scientific languages, and which in uniting them also relate them to that *Fact* which all the abstractive selections of scientific fact presuppose. Such a Fact we may well think demands "metaphysical" words, at any rate words lying outside the logic of science, but words in which the various scientific languages find together their unity, as well as each its completion, and applicability to Fact. For the moment we will say no more about this metaphysical supplement to the language of science, but having in mind the general character of scientific language as we have described it, we can readily see why there is no room for the word "miracle" within it.

Any ostensibly irregular features to which the word "miracle" has traditionally referred, and for our particular purpose we need not now specify the various sorts of nonconformity by examples, could never be treated in such language as is used by science. They could only at most be an occasion for expansibility or convertibility. To treat them in scientific language is either to ignore or to dissolve away all irregular features as the very condition of linguistic inclusion. This, of course, has in fact been the way miracle-features have been treated when miracles have been dealt with in scientific language. When prisons were opened or a tomb was empty, earthquakes were looked for or mistakes of memory invoked; when miraculous feeding took place, food was being handed round at the back, or perhaps nervous satisfaction created, or perhaps the natural processes of bread-making speeded up; healings were rather like hypnotic cures and so on. It is always fascinating to see how far, granted ingenuity and patience, more or less scientific language can go in its endeavour to be comprehensive.

But no matter how far it goes, the conclusion could never be that there are no miracles. We could never conclude more than that "miracle" had no place in scientific language. Indeed, there is no "conclusion" about it; the scientist is bound, as a condition of using scientific words, to exclude "miracle" from the start. All talk about the laws of nature is in the case of miracles a sheer waste of breath: whether or not they are broken is a pseudo-question. The word "break" cannot be used of "law" as it occurs in the logic of science. When scientific laws are generalizations at different abstractive levels, when they are more or less tentative directives of procedure, then scientific language can have no place for "miracle", and the less we embroil ourselves in irrelevant scientific discussion the better.

Of course, if scientific language were the only language and were itself all-sufficient, we might at this point find ourselves with the great embarrassment of a Newton who on the one hand wanted to believe in God and pretty certainly in miracles, and yet also had to work towards a uniform overall expansion of scientific language. Since he was unable to envisage more than one brand of language, the word "God" had then to work like a high-grade scientific concept, and had somehow to cover both scientific regularities and miraculous interventions, whereupon any gain in comprehensiveness was at once outweighed by the loss of consistency. Hence arose various puzzlements such as how God's constancy on the one hand could indeed be reconciled with his particular miraculous concern on the other. If miraculous concern really violated the constancy which belongs to God's moral concern, could it be other than capricious? And so on.

This difficulty of wanting God both for constancy and miraculous intervention has, in our own day, been formulated much more precisely and much more generally: can "God" sentences such as these ever be falsified, and if not are they even meaningful, let alone true? If events follow a regular pattern (it is said) we speak of God's "constant control". It might be expected then that should any irregularity occur, the assertion would be falsified. But not so. When events show irregularity, we speak of God's miraculous "intervention" as well. The result is a quite useless "hypothesis" without any honest empirical relevance. The God hypothesis (the story continues) has a "heads-I-win, tails-you-lose" character about it; there can be no genuine falsification, no genuine discussion about it, no genuine meaning in it. What is the cash-value, it is asked, of this concept "God" which is retained even when compromised by the most contradictory qualifications? Come what may, the argument says, all sorts of stories—including inconsistent ones—will be told, but the word "God" will be retained. "God" is everywhere, only because "God" means nothing anywhere.

The importance of this falsification puzzle is that it reminds us that the word "God" does not work as a high-grade scientific word at all. It is *not* part of a "hypothesis". God-sentences do not belong to the logic of science. But if our discussion of the limitations of scientific language has any truth in it, this does not necessarily exclude the possibility that "God" might have another logic altogether and be significant in an altogether different way. "God" might be something like what Russell would call another "logical type". It is indeed this fundamental difference in the logical geography of scientific words and "God" which the falsification puzzle underlines, and the only lesson we have to learn is that the word "God" when introduced must be given some *other* sort of empirical justification. We must tell an empirical tale quite different from the sort which accompanies a scientific sentence. The word "God" may well have empirical relevance, but this distinctive relevance will never be displayed by working it in a scientific sentence. For the word has another logical status altogether.

To meet the problem of non-falsification, to avoid the embarrassments of a Newton, and at the same time to make a possible defence of miracle, our next move will be to ask: What other language is there which has a structure different from scientific language? What other language is there in which the word "miracle" might fit? What language is there which refers to facts at a more concrete level than those which are described by science? Why not try history?

It is worth while emphasizing that not until the last century would this move have been even possible. For much of the seventeenth and eighteenth centuries there was thought to be only one brand of accurate language, viz. mathematics, and the pattern of historical language would have provided no genuine alternative option to the pattern of scientific language. Both in fact would have worked according to a Locke-Newton ideal. But as is well known, the nineteenth century brought a growing emphasis on the peculiarly distinctive character of historical "fact", and in saying what we shall do in the sequence, we are really trying to learn from this nineteenth-century concern with history and to unite it with a twentieth-century concern with language.

If then we try history, what shall we find as the broad features of historical language? What is there distinctive about its logic?

It might help us if at the start we try to elucidate the characteristic difference between the languages of science and history by two examples. Suppose we want to know, in the ordinary commonsense use of that word, about a Norfolk village, for example: its life in the past; its character to-day; its likely future. Forgetting altogether for the moment our concern with logical maps we might provide ourselves with a series of maps of different scales, each giving a greater and greater coverage but at the expense of

an Exercise in Logical Mapwork

describing fewer and fewer facts as the scale increased. Our understanding of the village in terms of all these maps might be compared to the sort of understandings that are possible by scientific languages. Alternatively, we might go blindfold to the village postmaster or policeman, uncover our eyes before him, listen to his talk and put two and two together and make six, or because that is an unfortunate expression (confusing as it does mathematical and historical language) let us say that we might from his talk put all sorts of vivid impressions together, and at some quite concrete level know and become conversant with the life of the village yesterday and to-day, and with its likely character to-morrow. Such a technique would be comparable to the function claimed for historical language. Despite its own particular inadequacies it would nevertheless give us our fullest and most comprehensive insight into the life of the village. What is portrayed would be an insight of the highest degree of concreteness.

To use another example, the languages of science and history might be seen as two techniques for talking about a cake. One would talk about the whole cake in terms of certain features which characterize it *entirely* but are highly abstract: its weight, its circularity, and so on; the other, *on the basis of a certain section*, would generalize about the whole, e.g. its mixing and baking in the past, its taste in the present, its likely contribution to my well-being in the future. This second sort of knowledge would obviously be less inadequate than the first as a clue to what "eating the cake" means. Eating the cake would, of course, if the word "concrete" in relation to cakes be pardoned, be an occurrence altogether more concrete than any picture-fact like circularity; it would even be more concrete than a picture-fact made up of those objective features which characterized any sectional wedge.

Building on these examples, we may now suggest that historical language is a technique for naming and organizing *at a concrete level of personal encounter*, such a selection of facts as endeavours to repeat certain "events as they occurred", and thus to bring them into relation with contemporary experience. True, there are several varieties of history—constitutional history, economic and social history, historical geography, and so on—but I would still assert that what is most distinctive about historical language, what distinguishes it from law or economics or geography, when the distinctive features of those languages have been severally elucidated, is that history is pre-eminently concerned with *persons*. Its distinctive feature is to use person-words as part of its technique for comprehensiveness, to use person-patterns in its search for concreteness. Its language portrays a pattern of personal events as a clue to the totality, "past", "present", and even "future", which it tries to interpret.

This is true, I say, no matter what variety of history we care to mention. In the case, for example, of economic history the word "person" will be worked in terms of the language of economics, i.e. a person will be a "hand", a "wage-earner", a "capitalist", and so on. But what, then, are we to say about history pure and simple? Is it something quite different from half-breeds like constitutional history or economic history?

To answer this question we must take our account of historical language somewhat farther, and there are two points to notice:

1. The pattern of personal events which constitutes the origin of some particular historical language must be a good clue to other events which surround them, and of which they are meant to be an indicator. The pattern must in other words have the necessary degree of *immediate relevance*. It is no use whatever going to the postmaster who only took office this morning, or taking a piece of cherry cake so cut (as I fear cherry cake nowadays can be cut) as to avoid a cherry. This is the matter of choosing evidence, and assessing the impressiveness of personalities.

2. Further, this originative pattern of personal events must be such as to give to the historical language in which it becomes expressed, the possibility of a wide extension. The pattern, in other words, must be *significant*. It is no use whatever going to the postmaster if no one uses the post office, or taking a piece of cake which, for example, is so small that you cannot tell whether it is a segment of an elliptical or a circular cylinder, or even of a triangular wedge.

The two points it is clear are really one. The *selection* which possesses original *relevance*, when once it is made, of itself provides for the *extension* and *significance*.

So historical language does not gain its extension by the scientific techniques of expansibility and convertibility. It does not gain its comprehensiveness by relating to ever more and more *abstract uniformities*. Here is a language with quite a different logic from the logic of science. It certainly seeks an insight into "all that happened", it makes a leap to total description—but this search for comprehensiveness is, for history, made at a concrete personal level. In history we are not concerned with abstract uniformities but with a *concrete* level of *personal* transactions. Historical language secures this concrete reference not only because its original selection is made at this level but also because in expanding its range it takes care to maintain the concreteness of the original selection. History is pre-eminently a technique for securing from a selected "clue" an extended insight at a concrete personal level.

But how, we may next ask, do we select the "clue" which provides for the extension? How is the original relevance determined, and so the significance secured? We have already had hints for an answer. Half-breed historical language takes this framework (of selection and extension) from elsewhere—from law, economics, geography, and so on; and then works person-words in these languages.

Generalizing, I would suggest that *all* historical language uses language from elsewhere to give such a setting to the word "person" as shall determine for a particular case the original selection of facts, and at the same time secure the possibility of extension. It uses language from elsewhere to make what Whitehead and others have called its judgement of "importance". Only from another sort of language altogether does the language of history find its necessary means of selection and extension at a personal level. History takes an outline pattern from another language, and, with this outline range and survey, constructs its personal pictures. It is not surprising then—indeed it is altogether expected—that there will be many historical half-breeds such as those we have noticed, i.e. historical geography, economic history, scientific history, resulting from this dependence of history on a non-historical language. Incidentally, to say, for example, that history is a science and neither more nor less, is merely to claim that there is only one satisfactory language model, i.e. "science", so that the historian, in his endeavours at selection and extension, is *bound* to use this pattern and no other. But as we have already seen, scientific language is something neither perfect nor homogeneous:

it has its inadequacies and its varieties, and there is no need for anyone searching for a language pattern to be restricted by some one of many merely outline sketches. Indeed, "scientific history" pays an unjustified compliment to science at the expense of historical slavery.

But to come back to the question we first raised a little time ago, what, on this background, is "history, pure and simple"? If history pure and simple needs a prior language technique as much as half-breed history, from where will it be derived? My suggestion is: from that language of maximum concreteness in which what we shall call the metaphysical index is most evident; more briefly, but less accurately: from metaphysics. Here is the measure of truth in the assimilation of history to philosophy. History can only succeed in the concrete endeavour it sets itself by having (before it begins) a map of the largest possible scale, a metaphysical viewpoint. Even with the village postmaster or policeman we have to know beforehand that the village is a community of persons.

If scientific language were at no point found to be inadequate, then scientific history would be the best history. If economics could give a completely satisfactory language map, then economic history would have the finality which some of its more enthusiastic supporters would like to give it. Our counter-claim is that history will attain its most concrete insights and generalize itself most adequately only when the language instrument it uses for its technique is least disguisedly metaphysical. But this brings us once more to the whole question of the status of metaphysical words, and we shall now turn to a few remarks in defence of metaphysics.

The need for metaphysical words has so far arisen in two ways:

1. The various languages of science (we suggested) need a metaphysical supplement (i) to complete each in the sense of "answering" "limiting questions", and (ii) so to unite all; and also (iii) to raise their various abstractive patterns to that level of concreteness which belongs to the "given fact" the languages intend to picture.

2. The most comprehensive historical language (i.e. that historical language least limited by the limitations of the language instrument it incorporates) needs a metaphysical viewpoint (rather than science or economics or geography) as its instrument of selection and extension.

In each of these two ways metaphysical words might be pictured

an Exercise in Logical Mapwork 15

as "marginal words" to any language map, and if we develop this suggestion a little farther we might notice that in some cases (and this resembles scientific language) these words are *wholly* written on the margins, e.g. "To Reading", "To Banbury", "To Ely", "To Norwich". In other cases (and this is more like the case of historical language which uses only part of a complete metaphysical matrix) part of a word, e.g. "BERK", may be written in the margin while the rest, e.g. "SHIRE", may be used in and occur on the map itself.

With this picture in mind the further, and perhaps rather obvious, point may now be made that the possibility of having one language map—the possibility of any sort of synthetic view of the world—when the occurrence of languages with many logics is admitted, depends on the possibility of these various marginal words being united in one group, to constitute one matrix. The suggestion is, that only if such a common presupposed metaphysical unit can be elucidated can we justify the variety of languages in their claim to be descriptions of One World—and I not only agree with Professor Ryle that there are not two worlds, but also go, I think, farther and claim that neither are there (say) fifty-seven varieties of world corresponding to the number of languages we may discover, each having its own logic. I am taking it as common ground that there are many languages each with its own logic (or meta-logic). We have looked at languages from two groups—science and history. In regard to these we have seen that they each require, though in different ways, words with a different logic altogether. I am now suggesting more generally that it is the task of metaphysics both to organize the supply of all these supplementary words and at the same time to collect the simplest possible number of them to fulfil their task as ultimate co-ordinators, and then to offer the resultant group as a sort of index to the total language scheme, which comprises both the index and the subordinate languages with their several logics.

So arises the idea of metaphysical words as co-ordinating, boundary, or index words uniting all the several languages, each of which has its own particular logic. Subordinate languages then occur within one total language system, in which the metaphysical words may (for example) round off some particular subordinate language (like a "boundary") or perhaps assist in the matter of factual reference (like an "index"). The curious language which makes up the index we might call (if Greek would permit it) a *Kata-language*, whose words can be used, and in various ways, in all the subordinate languages, though they can belong to the logic of none. They are consequently revealed by their permanent irreducibility, by the permanent puzzles to which they lead. But that is a point we cannot now take farther. Nor can we do more than mention the possibility that this metaphysical group of words may have a sort of presiding word or apex.

Another complication we cannot now clear up and which we only notice for the sake of clarity, so as to help guard against possible confusion, is that though there are really two senses in which a word might be said to be metaphysical, the first I shall mention is the sense which is distinctive and important:

1. Words may be metaphysical in the sense of belonging to the "index" of a language hierarchy and so to no one level, though they can be used (we have urged) at all levels of language. Such words are (we shall see) "I" and "God".

2. Words may be metaphysical as belonging to that language of maximum generalization which endeavours to do most justice to concrete fact—the top-level language of a language hierarchy, at which level the metaphysical index is most prominent. This would be the language of most traditional works on metaphysical philosophy.

To take just one specific example, I believe that all languages will throw up the word "activity" as being a word demanded by any particular language L_r, but not one which works according to L_r logic. Without going into detail I would claim that the traditional puzzles philosophers have found about activity, e.g. the problems of Movement, Change, Cause, Will, and so on, have really arisen from an attempt to work the word "activity" by an inadequate model instead of recognizing that it is a word presupposed (so I would suggest) at all language levels. The very puzzles, indeed, should be seen for what they are—witnesses to a misuse of words at the start. Not only do they confuse language-levels but they allow for no index independent of all levels. From another direction, not the least significant comment on the present epistemological turmoils of physics is that they indicate the desire to work with a primitive like "activity" rather than with the grammar of "passive-subject: independent-object". "Activity" then, we might

an Exercise in Logical Mapwork

argue, is a metaphysical word demanded for all languages and capable in particular of uniting the languages of science. It is a word which thus belongs to the metaphysical index.

But before leaving the question of metaphysical words to take up again the question of miracles, there is one further point we must develop in some detail. What of the applicability of the total system including the metaphysical index? Has the total system any sort of empirical relevance other than that which is derivative and secured through a subordinate language? Can the metaphysical words express nothing but an attitude towards, a "policy" in regard to, the subordinate languages and their related facts? To answer that sort of question I must play the card I laid on the table at the start; I must begin to eat the cake that so far I have merely described. For as all maps presuppose a country to be lived in, we are now really asking what is the territory of which our over-all language map proffers a description, and in particular what sort of territory is indicated by metaphysical words.

The total territory is clearly one which includes ourselves as well as all else. So, like Bradley's "Absolute" and for not dissimilar reasons, the territory our complete map proffers to describe seems to set the mapper a task he can never fulfil. What are we to do about it?

1. As a first move let us notice where, for example, in X's experience at any one time there lies this area that is not publicized, and which sets the mapper his unenviable task. We might say it is the area called "I_x" as distinct from the "me_x". However many mistakes may have been made in models for Privileged Access, we still have the privilege of being ourselves, and public though we may be, each of us recognizes that he is not so public as to be lost in the crowd. In every situation, when "I" and "me" have been distinguished, "I" cannot be given an exhausitive "objective" analysis without denying ourselves in fact, or without supposing that the subject-object relation in language is merely the subject-predicate relation, which seems a quite unnecessary, indeed a quite disastrous, assumption. It is what Whitehead calls "extreme objectivism" which even objectifies the subject.

2. On the other hand, we might readily admit that "me", as commonly used, often denotes something as public as anyone would wish. "The fellow you saw running for the bus yesterday?

That was me" may be bad English, but it is often good philosophy. "Me" = "that fellow running" = "those muscles strained, that mouth blowing" is something to which there is for all of us public access. Not so "I", either at the time or now. "I" eludes public gaze, yesterday, to-day, and to-morrow. But what then, it will be said, does "I" refer to? If "I" can never be "objectified" — but always (if the question is raised) distinguished from an objective "me" — surely it can never be talked about. Hardly. All we can say is, it cannot be talked about in terms of languages of ordinary "observational" logic: it cannot be talked about in terms of what we have called a "subordinate language". It will belong to a language of curious logic indeed; but there is nothing disreputable about that if this language is necessitated by the facts.

3. The problem is, first, how to indicate these "facts" that demand "I"? Clearly it will only be done in a curious way. To do it thoroughly in a particular case we should have to recall for someone examples of all sorts of situations they could recognize, e.g. occasions of veridical perception, of hallucination, of moral judgements, of "religious experience", and so on: the more varied the better. We might then say that "I" referred to that common element in which they would find that these various and varying recallings agreed. "I" refers to that which *all* the situations would include, each in its peculiar setting. It is, to say, the cone of which each language is concerned to portray some "specific" conic section. Though our patient might be intractable, the experiment would have to go on until there was a cone-disclosure.

4. Having now established the *facts*, the problem is, next, to find the appropriate language for their treatment. The suggestion is that, as a first approximation, which also recalls the importance we have already given to the word "activity", we might try "I actively related to me": and if we wanted to describe the conclusion of the experiment included in 3 we would then have to say that it induced awareness of "I actively related to me". But clearly this is precisely where the language difficulty returns. To be aware *of* "I actively related to me" suggests that "I actively related to me" is an "objective" fact, and it was precisely this we wished to deny. How, then, can we avoid the difficulty at this second move? Only by saying (*a*) that the conclusion of the experiment in 3 is an "awareness", clearly non-inferential at any rate, which must be

given, in some sense, subject–object components as a condition of ever talking about it and so setting it in a language framework. (b) We would then add that "I actively related to me" is recommended as a "description" — to a first approximation — of that subject–object awareness. The phrase would thus be commended as "useful nonsense" involving words with a new logic.

My suggestion so far is that for each of us "I" is one of our key metaphysical words, and that in the relation of "I" to "me" we have the clue for relating the metaphysical index to the rest of language. Further, I am suggesting that the factual justification for "I" in particular, and metaphysical words in general, is given in a non-inferential awareness more concrete than cognition. For cognition, as Hume so rightly claimed, yields only "objective" data, and must always end by trying to substitute in the case of each and all of us a public "me" for a unique "I". Incidentally, it is notable that Berkeley had to complete a (Humean) theory of public "ideas" with a doctrine of curious "notions" to account for the language we use significantly about the activity of ourselves and the external world.

5. But one last and further point must yet be made. We have spoken hitherto of a "first approximation", and we have urged that "I" has its public counterpart in "me" which characterizes the Other. Then may it not be plausible to suppose that, as the logic of "me" implies another logic for "I", so also observation-logic about "individuals" or "other people" implies another logic for "person"? "Person" would be that word used of those situations which, at one level, use "other people" logic, but for which a complete description demand in addition a counterpart-word for "I" and find it in "person". To express the point differently, the word "person" would then characterize the subject–object awareness *objectively* at the same level of language, at the same level of concretion, as "I" characterizes it *subjectively*. We may represent the argument as follows:

20   *Miracles*

Start: "subject–object awareness" recommended as a label for a certain situation.
Then, as a first development of a language map:
"I actively related to me"
A second development of a language map:

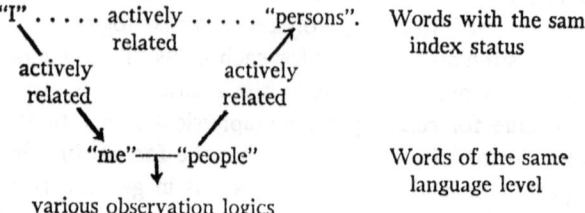

various observation logics

So, with 1 to 5 in mind, we might say that the territory of which our overall map proffers a description is a territory revealed by a non-inferential awareness induced in the way we have hinted; and that the part of that territory to which metaphysical words are appropriate and by which these are necessitated is the residue left when the subordinate languages have each and all claimed their "objective" data.

Incidentally, may we not claim some support in all this from Professor Ryle? In *The Concept of Mind*, pp. 50-51, he says (italics mine): "When a *person* talks sense aloud, ties knots . . . [then he] . . . is bodily active and he is mentally active, but he is not being synchronously active in two different "places" or with two different "engines". There is the *one activity*, but it is one susceptible of and requiring more than one kind of explanatory description." Is not this to imply that the phrase "personal activity" has a logic all its own but that it can nevertheless be related to "more than one kind of explanatory description", that is, that the facts can be described by a variety of subordinate languages with logics of more than one sort? It is, I think, not without significance that when Professor Ryle so strikingly and ingeniously unpacks so much into observation sentences yet there is nevertheless a phrase like "personal activity" (i.e. "activity" when attached to some personal situation) which seems to be a phrase seeking for another sort of logic altogether. Then again, in this matter of "person" we might note the tautology which Professor Ryle asserts on p. 81: "Men are not machines, not even ghost-ridden machines. They are men—a tautology which is sometimes worth remembering." Such a tautology we might say is,

an Exercise in Logical Mapwork

again, "useful nonsense", and has the function of recommending "man"–"person" as a metaphysical word. Taking both quotations together we might claim that they suggest at any rate that "personal activity" is a phrase belonging to a metaphysical index of the kind we have been trying to defend.

Metaphysical words are, then, more than a pious jingle of "regulative" words, because they are that part of a language system whose empirical necessity arises from the fact that experience is not exhaustively described in terms of any number of parts which are "objective" in any number of senses. The ultimate justification of metaphysical words lies in the fact that there is a non-inferential awareness more concrete than the observable facts which characterize it abstractly and objectively. Metaphysical words are, then, related in a curious way to the residue; and any *total* language map relates at once to the concrete non-inferential awareness and to the "data" which are abstractively discernible. Further, if what we have said is true, it is clear then that "I" and "person" are metaphysical words in our sense.

Having this view of metaphysics in mind, and recollecting our view of historical language and its dependence on metaphysics, let us now ask, in relation to historical language, whether "miracle" has any place in it.

Without going into any great detail we might say that an event is a miracle (*a*) when it is in some obvious way "non-conforming" – a *"miraculum"*, and (*b*) when it is thereby a sign – a σημεῖον – as well; a sign traditionally of God's power, very often, in particular, of his kindness, and so on. Thus from the historical point of view a miracle is an event of great *relevance* and *significance*; a focal event which somehow demands description in terms of God's activity. Now after what we have said about metaphysics providing for history its instrument both of selection and of extension, by which relevance and significance are given to its focal events, it is clear that this amounts to saying that if the word "miracle" is to have any place in historical language, miracles must be events which carry theism as a metaphysical framework. They must be events (so to say) with their metaphysical labels on them, and in particular the word "God". So the question: Can we place "miracle" anywhere on our language map? becomes: Can we place "God's activity" anywhere on our language map?

The first suggestion we make is that "God" be introduced as the metaphysical apex of our language system, whose relation to the subordinate languages, and whose broad empirical relevance, is gained in a not un-Berkeleyan manner by relating it to the word "independent" as used of the existence of physical objects. In this way it would illuminate and interpret the word "independent" and incorporate it into the total language system, by uniting it with the word "activity", and so would fulfil a task of co-ordination and synthesis in a distinctively metaphysical manner:

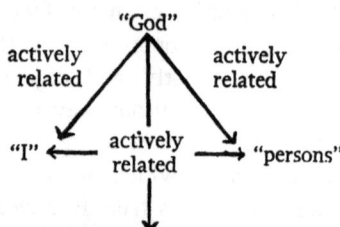

"independent" as used of the existence of physical objects

On this view, the claim of the Ontological Argument for God as the most perfect Being which necessarily exists would be rather a claim for "God" as the unique apex of the language hierarchy necessary to give that hierarchy or map that finitude which the possibility of its "reasonable" or "explanatory" use demands. The Cosmological argument in claiming total dependence on God would be claiming that the concept of God's activity provided a final—apex—explanation of any and every existent, but if it spoke of this activity as a "first cause" (as it often does) it would have to distinguish this carefully from scientific causation. And so on.

For our present purpose the next important point is that God's activity can be specified in two ways. "God", as we have now introduced the word, can be properly spoken of as *both* "active" (in relation to an "independent external world") *and* as "personally active" (in relation to "I" and "persons"). Let us see if we can illuminate this distinction by some examples.

On the one hand, we can all recognize that *general* activity which characterizes us and the world in all ordinary perceptual situations, and which, for example (to an observer), still characterizes us in dreamless sleep. It is that general activity which James

Ward called "conation" or (in one sense) "faith". It is, indeed, not unlike the "conatus" of Spinoza.

On the other hand, we equally well recognize that *particularized* activity which further characterizes us and the world in those special situations, involving ourselves and other people, which we call "love" or "personal devotion". Of course, sometimes such "love" or "personal devotion" may be given to a place or a thing, e.g. to a college or (in the case of a schoolboy) to a new bicycle, but I think it is clear that this is a derivative use of the word which, while of importance, need not detain us now. What we are suggesting is that there is an empirical difference to be discerned in the activity of ourselves and our environment which we might call one of "degree" or "order".

The distinction I have in mind might also be exemplified by considering doctor–patient or judge–prisoner situations. Normally, the events constituting the active encounter would be described in terms of scientific or legal language, and the patient or the prisoner would be just part of the objective environment abstracted for immediate attention according to the techniques of scientific or legal language. Nor would "the doctor" or "the judge" refer to more than a group of publicly accessible data. Of course, if a scientific language (and for now we will leave legal language aside) has a possible supplement of metaphysical words (as we have urged it will have), then in a *complete* description there would have to be a reference to God's activity as well. This would be that activity which in traditional theology would be said to sustain and conserve the universe, the activity which is "prevenient grace", and so on. But that is another point which we will mention again in a moment. Meanwhile we will return to our example.

Suppose now that all medical etiquette and law court customs were, on a certain occasion, broken, so that the patient was the doctor's wife and the prisoner the judge's wife, to which wives doctor and judge are respectively devoted, then for a full description of events which constitute the active encounter there would now be needed, besides scientific and legal language, other language as well—the intimate familiarities of family nicknames and all those words and varieties of descriptions that seem to the outsider so sentimental, far-fetched, unreasonable, and so on. What I am suggesting is that this different and curious language witnesses to a significant empirical difference between the two situations which we describe by saying that in the second case there is a *personal* encounter. The very nicknames we use are in their peculiarity a crude attempt to give to "person" the status of a metaphysical index: to do some justice to that concrete encounter of which we are non-inferentially aware, and which is never exhausted by the more sober and scientific subordinate languages.

What I want to say is that this empirical difference can be more systematically expressed in terms of two "orders" of activity. I want to argue that there is always a "first-order" activity which characterizes ourselves and the whole of our environment and for whose description "scientific" language will be appropriate. But in the case of certain special situations I suggest that a "second-order" activity as well characterizes ourselves and some appropriate part of the environment, an activity which demands for its description words of another logic altogether—indeed, the metaphysical word "person". But notice that there is neither a split in our personalities nor a split in the environment. Within our own activity we make a distinction of "order" which can be represented roughly as that between "me-active" and "I-active". We then transfer this distinction to our environment. It is a distinction between "general" activity and "personal" activity, a distinction which can be expressed alternatively as one between "first-order" activity and "second-order" activity.

But always, whether it is in regard of ourselves or our environment, or both, there is, as Ryle says, only "one activity", and "one world". Indeed, this claim for "one activity" and "one world" is really (we would say) a claim for "one" as a metaphysical apex word. It is the claim that despite the many empirically distinguishable characteristics and activities everything is "one", which means that the word "one" is operative and paradoxical at all language levels. This alone would suggest its metaphysical status, and by its uniqueness it seems, further to come near to being a metaphysical apex. Ryle's claim for "one" thus closely resembles our claim for "God". To forget the point about "one world" and "one activity" is not only, Cartesian-like, to split both the universe and our personalities. On our view it would also be to split God and, more particularly (as will be evident), it would also split off miracles from natural events. There is, then, "one" activity and we would say "God's"

an Exercise in Logical Mapwork 25

activity; yet at the same time, for our present purpose an important empirical distinction must be made (we have urged) between two "orders": God's "first-order" activity and "second-order" activity. His "first-order" activity would be that activity for whose description the logic of science is appropriate. His "second-order" (or personal) activity, if and when it occurred, would need rather, we should expect, the logic of history, and be indicated in the empirical patterns appropriate to, and suggested by, historical techniques.

The suggestion which comes out of all this is that the word "miracle" is a word in the logic of (metaphysical) history which is used to describe an event which witnesses to, and is an occasion of, a *personal, second-order* activity of God, of which we are in some basic and non-inferential sense directly aware. A miracle is an historical event which, *a fortiori* demanding for its description "personal activity", needs also the description "God". The difficulty of mapping the word "miracle" is, then, precisely the difficulty of having the words "personal activity" *and* the word "God" used of an event treated historically.

Taking a little farther the point of "grace" we mentioned above, a miracle as an occasion of second-order activity becomes in traditional language an occasion not only of "prevenient grace" but also of "co-operative grace". It is the special and further claim of a New Testament miracle that the second-order activity it exhibited was unique: that here was an occasion of "the grace of the Lord Jesus Christ".

Having now seen something of the far-reaching implications of this problem, the main conclusion may perhaps be represented as follows:

The Phrase:	belongs to:	In relation to which must be placed:
1. Me-active	scientific language	God "generally" active; God's "first-order" activity = "providence", a word in the theological supplement to science.
2. I-active	metaphysical language	God "personally" active; God's "second-order" activity = "miracle", a word of (metaphysical) history.

Incidentally, we may now easily see (though in detail it would be another story) why talk about causation and scientific laws has bedevilled not only discussions about miracles but also discussions about "Free Will". In both cases there has been the same sort of language blunder in ever letting such discussions begin—the same confusion of languages with different logics. For while determinism, like "providence", belongs to scientific language, "freedom", like "miracle", belongs to metaphysical language. The claim for "freedom", indeed, is no more and no less than the claim we have made for the phrase "personal activity", that it has metaphysical ultimacy, and "miracle" makes a free-will claim about the universe.

The striking character of miracles is thus to be related to their historical significance and extension and not at all to their scientific illegality, which is, indeed, a pseudo-category. It was a true insight of St Paul to indicate the miraculous character of the Incarnation by setting it within that historical pattern which in the Old Testament was a story of the Remnant and in the New Testament the story of the Christian Church. He was, albeit unconsciously, giving to Christian miracles their proper significance—as key events giving, and given in terms of, historical extensions.

Let us endeavour to summarize the main points in the lecture like this. Suppose we are asked the straightforward question, "Do miracles occur?" This question, we have now seen, cannot be a scientific question. "Do miracles occur?" does not work like "Does boiling water occur at 100°C.?", "Does oxygen occur?", or "Do electrons occur?", even allowing for all the different grades of scientific language which these last three questions imply. The so-called conflict between science and miracles is a pseudo-conflict which only arises when complete adequacy is claimed for the language of science. Of course, this is not by itself to defend miracles. It is only to say that if the word "miracle" has a logical setting it will not be found in the logic of science. So in our consideration of the question we looked elsewhere and passed to historical language.

"Do miracles occur?", when regarded as a question of historical language, is no doubt better formulated as "On such and such an occasion did a miracle 'M' occur?", and this last question can be analysed into three others.

1. The first question is one which, traditionally, would be said to be the question of "evidence" for 'M'. But "evidence" is a word of which we might well beware, since if we are not extraordinarily

an Exercise in Logical Mapwork 27

careful it will deceive us at this second move into thinking that the logic of history is the logic of science. What concerns us in this question is rather the explication of "M" with reference to (*a*) its historical selection and (*b*) its historical extension. The bare question as to whether some event "M" did, or did not, occur, is to be answered more, or less, affirmatively according as to whether "M" does, or does not, give a stable historical insight which never loses, but gains, significance and relevance as other events (of course in other settings) are adduced. For example, the reason why there is "better evidence" for a miracle story told in each of the four gospels is not that it is, scientific-like, four times as plausible as if it were only told in one, but rather that the pattern of events for which "M" is significant and relevant increases in four directions at once as four different and consistent stories are told. So much, then for this first question.

2. But if ever we give an affirmative answer to the question, "On such and such an occasion, did a miracle 'M' occur?" we are also commending theism as a particular Kata-language, a particular metaphysical index. This Kata-language would be commended in saying of a certain event that it was a "miracle", in so far as theistic "marginal" or "index" words were used by the historical framework in which the particular event was set. Expressed otherwise, in saying of an event that it is a "miracle" we are in part commending a map which includes metaphysical words, and in particular the phrase "God's second-order (or personal) activity".

3. Remembering what we have said about the applicability of metaphysical words, we should also be claiming that the event "M" occurred within a peculiar sort of empirical situation. We should, indeed, be making the claim (to take as an example the simplest case of nature miracles) that there are groups of empirical facts to which the word "person" is *not* normally applied which nevertheless demand for their description the word "person" and in particular the word "God". The word "miracle", that is, is a metaphysical word to name and characterize those empirical situations when our non-inferential awareness cannot be adequately described in any language which does not extend to, and link together, the words "personal (second-order) activity" and the word "God".

The questions we may usefully ask about a miracle are, then, not scientific questions at all, but are such questions as the following:

1. Have we examined, as far as in us lies, as much "evidence" as possible, i.e. original documents, traditional doctrine, and so on?

2. Is theistic Kata-language the most adequate Kata-language available, and hence justified for methodological use by history? Are the metaphysical words which theism offers to us adequate as a co-ordinating and presiding index? To deal with that sort of question is, I need hardly say, a lifetime's task for any of us.

3. Was the person, or persons, in the particular miracle-claiming situation justified in claiming that "God's personal activity" was needed fully to describe this non-inferential awareness? No doubt a relevant question would be whether we ourselves have a like need when the situation is recalled for us by the writer. This, of course, is to raise the whole question of "a living Word" and it is one which in the end each one of us can only answer, and in particular circumstances, for himself.

But let us not be misunderstood by that remark. Because we have laid stress on this non-inferential awareness both in our justification of metaphysics and miracle, we do not suggest that in the case of miracle there is some infallible or incorrigible claim: some private access which would lead to "enthusiasm" indeed. On the contrary, let me stress that besides this matter of non-inferential awareness, points (1) and (2) above must always be kept in mind, i.e. (1) historical "evidence" will need to be collected and compared with the greatest care, and in a search that never supposes it has ended. (2) Further, the concept of miracle is, we have seen, always linked with a particular index recommendation, and for this the overall test, and one to which it must continually be submitted, will be the simplicity, comprehensiveness, and coherence of the total language. We shall rightly be suspicious of any denial of miracles which comes because a particular metaphysical language has no room for the word, especially if that particular language is the result of trying to do metaphysics with one language model. But such philosophical blundering or prejudice must not blind religious people to the truth of a personally active God. They stand or fall together.

So we may properly remind ourselves of the wider setting in which this discussion about miracles has all along been set, and which we mentioned at the start. Not only have we tried to show

an Exercise in Logical Mapwork 29

how the conflict with science is a pseudo-conflict, or, more positively, to justify a use for the word "miracle" which gives it a distinctive place in historical language. We have also tried to set the word "miracle" on a total language map which includes a metaphysical index; a map by which all discursive knowledge (and as examples we have taken science and history) is integrated, and whose unity, on the view I have barely outlined, relates to the activity of God himself.

From another point of view, this comes to saying that we have preserved the distinctiveness of miracle not at the cost of some scientific scandal about empirical events, but by positing, on the basis of our experience of persons, a greater complication than we might have originally expected in the activity of God himself. Along with such a claim for God and his activity there has also arisen the possibility of a new language synthesis, a new unity of knowledge, a new over-all map by which to explore the universe. Nor does the devotional significance of all this need any stressing.

You might suppose, however, from most of the lecture, that this Chair was founded to enable simple questions to be so complicated as to ensure that the occupant should never be out of a job. It is true that none of us in these days needs apologize for finding simple questions complicated, but the suggestion constrains me to end with another general point lest it be supposed that I think religion nothing but an intellectual pastime.

If what I have urged is true, while we all bear in our mouths a language scheme more or less adequate, none is sacrosanct or unique. The task of all of us must be to search (so far as time and ability allow) for that language scheme which is most simple, comprehensive, and coherent. Meanwhile we must all use our total language—whether professor or tinker—with no illusions about its adequacy. After all, it is only a map to understand as best we can that of which we are non-inferentially aware, which is the Fact all of us are endeavouring all the time to understand and describe better. There is always, of course, the somewhat curious theoretical possibility that another total scheme will be found with another metaphysical index. So it is in one good sense of the word "faith" that we embrace any scheme we have, and also set it more concretely in such an experience as worship. For "worship" is the compact name conveniently given to our awareness of the two-ordered activity which confronts us. This is perhaps to say that there is, in the end, something not altogether unlike Wittgenstein's one-time mysticism, something like scientific wonder, something like religious faith, which is the justification for metaphysics in general and miracles in particular.

Flaws and inadequacies in our thinking will always remain. But let us take heart. That is as it should be. No inaugural lecture could be *designed* as the conclusion to our thinking, though unkind rumour has it that in some cases, which the past gracefully conceals, that has in *fact* proved to be the case. For the moment, however, we can rejoice that this inaugural lecture inaugurates the vacation — which is at least one encouraging reflection that those who have honoured me with their presence can now bear away.

© Ian T. Ramsey, 1952.

2

THE GOSPEL MIRACLES:
Views Past and Present [1]

G. H. BOOBYER

THE four canonical gospels contain many accounts of "mighty works" performed by Jesus. But in what sense are all these "mighty works" rightly called miracles—especially as they include such diverse achievements as exorcisms, the resurrection of the dead, the cure of paralysis, the withering of a fig tree, the healing of lepers, and the transformation of water into wine?

In his famous essay, "Of Miracles", David Hume defined a miracle as "a transgression of a law of nature by a particular volition of the Deity, or by the interposition of some invisible agent".[2] But if by definition "miracle" is to connote "a transgression of a law of nature", the word no longer remains a fitting comprehensive label for Christ's "mighty works". To be sure, some of these seem to imply transgressions of the commonly accepted laws of nature, particularly the miracles classified frequently as "nature miracles"—those like the multiplication of the loaves, the changing of water into wine at Cana, and the stilling of tempests, in all of which Jesus exercises power over some aspect of nature,

[1] This essay is a revised and extended version of an article which appeared in *The Friends' Quarterly*, Vol. 13, No. 7, July 1960, under the title "The Miracle-Narratives in the Gospels".

[2] Section x of *An Enquiry Concerning Human Understanding*, edited by Selby-Bigge, footnote 1, p. 115 (Clarendon Press, 2nd ed., 1902). T. H. Huxley, who shared Hume's scepticism about the value of the evidence for miracles (in the gospels or elsewhere), objected to the wording of this definition on the ground that it really implies "that which never has happened never can happen without a violation of the laws of nature", whereas we are never in a position to be able to assert this. See *Collected Essays*, by T. H. Huxley, Vol. VI, pp. 154-7 (Macmillan, 1894).

as distinct from persons. Yet in the light of modern medical knowledge, it would be foolish indeed to apply a term signifying transgressions of the known laws of nature to miracles like Jesus' exorcisms, cures of paralysis, restoration of sight, hearing, or speech, and some healings of physical illness. These may not involve such transgressions.

If, then, the word "miracle", understood entirely in Hume's sense, cannot be employed as comprehensively as we propose to use it, what meaning is here attached to the term? Etymologically, "miracle" (Latin *miraculum*) denotes an act, or an event, which evokes wonder. That is its basic significance. In what follows, however, "miracle" is mostly employed with a fuller connotation. It is generally meant to signify an achievement which evokes wonder, because the observers believe that it transcends what is humanly possible, that it is something inexplicable by ordinary knowledge of the world, and therefore implies the special operation of extraordinary or supernatural power. This use of "miracle" leaves the relation of any particular miracle to the laws of nature undetermined. It also expresses with sufficient accuracy the sense in which some of the deeds of Jesus were miracles to his first followers. This was fundamentally their meaning when, in their own language, they proclaimed Jesus of Nazareth as "a man approved of God unto you by mighty works and wonders and signs, which God did by him in the midst of you" (Acts 2. 22). As applied, therefore, to the "mighty works" of Jesus, "miracle" in the following discussion is but a traditional designation for certain extraordinary deeds of his to which the earliest Christians reacted with wonder, attributing them to the supernatural power of God operating in and through him. Thus the term is not intended to convey any prejudgement of the critical problems to which the miracle-stories give rise: it is not meant to suggest the adoption of either a credulous or a sceptical attitude to their historicity, or to the religious interpretation put upon them by the gospel writers. These are questions for examination, not for predetermination by an arbitrary use of terms.

It will help to put the whole subject a little in perspective, if we now take a brief glance at some of the attitudes taken to the miracles in the past.[3] From the days when he lived amongst men

[3] J. S. Lawton in *Miracles and Revelation* (Lutterworth Press, 1959) provides a comprehensive survey of the treatment of the gospel miracles

down to our time, Christ's claim to work miracles has been met with both belief and unbelief; and the sceptics are no new thing. Jesus himself was confronted with them. Some of them said that he cast out devils not by the help of the Spirit of God, but by Beelzebub, which was a way of equating his works with the works of Satan. In the second century, the pagan philosopher Celsus also used the miracles as a means of discrediting Jesus: they indicated, said Celsus, that the Christians' Christ was in fact a sorcerer who had learnt his art from Egyptian magicians. Origen's *Contra Celsum*, written in the third century, dealt with this charge. At the beginning of the fifth century, we find Augustine of Hippo addressing himself to those who rejected the gospel miracles on the ground that—so they said—no such miracles occurred in their own day.[4] But following the widespread credulity with which miracles were received in the earlier and later medieval Church came the period when they began to be assailed more widely and with more systematically argued attacks. The rationalistic and empirical philosophers of the seventeenth and eighteenth centuries formed the vanguard of this assault—thinkers like Spinoza, Hume, and the Deists. Finally, with nineteenth-century writers like Matthew Arnold and T. H. Huxley, sceptical views appear stiffened with knowledge drawn from progress in the natural sciences and biblical scholarship. Indeed, notwithstanding stout championship of the miracle-narratives in the gospels by churchmen such as R. C. Trench and J. B. Mozley, Christians themselves began to swell the ranks of the doubters. Matthew Arnold wrote *Literature and Dogma* and *God and the Bible* in the faith that "Christianity is immortal", that it possesses "a boundless future", and that whatever modern knowledge might say, men could still find the Bible a source of life and joy. But, said Arnold, this will remain true only if the thoughtful Bible reader is told "that in travelling through its reports of miracles he moves in a world, not of solid history, but of illusion, rumour and fairy-tale".[5] In short, although Jesus did on occasion cure

from the seventeenth century to the present day. The book also gives a full bibliography; and an enormous amount has been written about miracles from both the believing and the sceptical standpoints.

[4] See especially *The City of God*, Books xxi and xxii. [Everyman's Library contains a handy edition in two volumes, published in 1945.]

[5] *God and the Bible*, Popular Edition, Smith, Elder & Co., 1893, pp. 24f.

illness deriving from moral troubles, "miracles do not happen".[6]

This judgement provides a convenient and provocative point of departure for a reconsideration of some of the problems which the miracles attributed to Jesus present. Must we, like Matthew Arnold, still conclude that these narratives are fiction rather than fact and therefore bring embarrassment instead of help both to the Bible reader and to the Christian apologist? Or is a revision of Arnold's verdict possible in the light of the advances in science and biblical scholarship made in the present century? Since the gospels devote so much space to miracles—about one third of St Mark's Gospel is concerned with them—these questions are important. Contemporary theological scholarship shows awareness of this in the continuing vigour with which they are debated.

I

Let us begin with a look at the more negative side of the discussion —at those factors which in varying degrees seem to discredit either the historicity of the miracle-stories or their religious value.

For most people the presence of these narratives in the Bible is no longer of itself a strong guarantee of their historical reliability, inasmuch as the historical inerrancy of the Scriptures is a doctrine widely abandoned. Moreover, the biblical accounts of miracle do in themselves give difficulty. Where more than one evangelist reports the same miracle, discrepancies may be found which raise the observant reader's distrust. St Matthew, for instance, turns Mark's one Gadarene madman into two, and makes Jairus say to Jesus, "My daughter is even now dead" whereas Mark reports him as saying that she was "at the point of death". But the major problems at first sight are usually the following. Scientific difficulties emerge, since the miracle-narratives relate events like the resuscitation of dead bodies which seem at variance with the ordered behaviour of nature as science (or even our own experience) has revealed it. There are also the moral difficulties. So much in the Gospels depicts a Jesus incomparably great in moral and spiritual stature. It becomes incongruous, therefore, to find him cursing a fig tree for not bearing fruit when "it was not the season of figs", or destroying peasants' means of livelihood by sending devils into their swine!

[6] Preface to the Popular Edition of *Literature and Dogma*, published by Smith, Elder & Co., 1884, p. xii.

Confronted with what looks like the incredible, the reader may be inclined to write the miracles off, and forget them. But that would be superficial; nor can the Gospels be treated like this, if we are to understand the Christian religion. If there are problems, they must be faced. Thus the questions raised by the miracles call for further questions. How did these stories arise? What factors have influenced their transmission? What interpretation did the evangelists and their first readers put upon them? How much truth do they contain?

To-day, biblical scholars freely acknowledge that the accounts of the miracles in the gospels contain facts together with embellishments of facts and elements of fiction. But to what extent is fact mingled with fiction? That is always the question. And, naturally enough, in expounding any miracle-story different scholars give different answers. The difficulty is mostly that of rightly estimating the effects of the processes and influences to which these narratives were subject before assuming their present written form. The foundation of most of them lies in what originally happened, but the present content owes something to their treatment on the lines of transmission along which they have come to us, where various factors have affected them. What, then were these?

The handling of the gospel traditions during the first twenty or thirty years after the death of Jesus is, of course, a basic consideration. This was a period when these traditions existed mainly, it would seem, in oral forms, and much remained unwritten longer. Further, although the first Christians, like the Jews, will have had their methods of keeping oral traditions under some degree of disciplined control, they were human, as all men, and not immune from human limitations and proclivities. Hence a measure of spurious growth in the gospel traditions is unlikely to have been avoided. A confession once made by a scholarly American Quaker, Rufus M. Jones, illustrates the point. "Every person", he wrote, "however honest and morally qualified he may be, tends to enhance in the reporting, in the telling, a story that has a large element of the mysterious, the seemingly miraculous, about it . . . . I have myself found it necessary to stop telling certain striking incidents, for I caught myself *improving* them with the repeated telling."[7] Clear

---

[7] Foreword to *George Fox's "Book of Miracles"*, edited by Henry J. Cadbury, C.U.P., 1948, p. xii.

examples of "improvements" of the miracle stories made by early Christians appear in the apocryphal gospels. Let the reader but sample the version of the resurrection story provided by the second century Gospel of Peter, or the prodigies which the boy Jesus performed according to the Infancy Gospel of Thomas.[8] How far had this fictitive, "improving" process gone with some of the canonical miracle-stories before their inclusion in our New Testament gospels? Obviously, no one can be quite certain.

In addition to the human inclination to enhance the more sensational features of a story in the retelling, study has detected other formative tendencies and influences operative upon the gospel traditions in the period of their oral transmission. There is a possibility that sayings of Jesus were on occasion transformed into stories; that experiences originally connected with the resurrection of Jesus assumed the form of occurrences in the public ministry before the crucifixion; and that the contents of the Old Testament helped to develop and even to create miracle stories. Is, for example, the cursing of the fig tree a dramatization of the parable of the unfruitful fig tree (Luke 13. 6-9)? There are scholars who think so. Was the miraculous draught of fishes reported in Luke 5. 1-11 an event at first connected with an appearance of Jesus to his disciples after the resurrection? Some expositors see a suggestion of it in points of contact between this passage and the narrative recorded in John 21. 1-14. And how far has the Old Testament fashioned narratives like the feeding of the five thousand, the stilling of tempests, and the raising of the dead?[9] Many judge their debt to the Old Testament to be real, although even a radical critic such as R. Bultmann considers that it is frequently overemphasized.[10] That parallels to the gospel miracle-stories appear in pagan circles where Old Testament influence is not to be assumed, would seem to justify Bultmann's *caveat*, even though Christians in the apostolic age were eager to show fulfilments of the Old Testament in their Lord's teaching and work.

Something should now be added about miracles in the non-

[8] These apocryphal works can be read in *The Apocryphal New Testament*, edited by M. R. James, O.U.P., 1924.

[9] O.T. passages often cited for their influence on such miracle-narratives are Ex. 16. 4, 13-15; 2 Kings 4. 42-44; Ps. 65. 7; Job 9. 8; 1 Kings 17. 17-24; 2 Kings 4. 17-37, etc.

[10] Cf. *Geschichte der synoptischen Tradition*, 2 Aufl., 1931, pp. 245f.

Christian world of New Testament times. The Old Testament and Judaism in the New Testament period related miracles, and the Graeco-Roman world provided them in plenty. The temple of Asclepius at Cos has been described as "a veritable pagan Lourdes";[11] and miracles in profusion were reported of personalities like Pythagoras, Simon Magus, and Apollonius of Tyana, or of men of affairs such as the emperor Vespasian. In the third century, a certain Hierocles (a provincial governor under Diocletian) even wrote a book to show that Apollonius (first century A.D.) had as good a claim as Christ to esteem as a sage and miracle-worker. Moreover, as in the gospels, so too in the contemporaneous non-Christian world one hears of the healing of physical disablement and disease, miraculous feedings, walking on water, stilling storms, changing water into wine, and the raising of the dead to life.[12] There is no good reason to suppose extensive Christian borrowing from such non-Christian tales, but their study throws light on the mentality of the times. Men readily saw unusual happenings as marvels, prodigies, and portents. This was a natural consequence of their limited knowledge of the processes of the physical universe and of their "theology"—their views of the character and behaviour of the supernatural beings who controlled nature and man. Thus Augustine of Hippo could regard it as a miracle that a loadstone drew iron and that lime "burnt" in water. Nor did he have reason to doubt that sheer prodigies occurred, because God is almighty, and "as God can create what he will, so can he change the nature of what he has created at his good pleasure".[13] For Augustine, therefore, it was a corollary of his conception of God's omnipotence that miracles and prodigies could happen; and the attitude of the first two generations of Christians will have been much the same.

Here we must leave our review of the main processes and influences which played some part in making the miracle-narratives found in the gospels what they now are. But how great a part? That is, of course, the main question, and, as has been already indicated,

[11] *Jesus, Master and Lord*, H. E. W. Turner, Mowbray, 1954, p. 163.
[12] For examples of such non-Christian miracles and a fuller discussion of their bearing on the miracles in the gospels, see M. Dibelius, *From Tradition to Gospel*, 1934, especially chapter vi; R. Bultmann, *Geschichte der synoptischen Tradition*, 1931, pp. 247-253; R. M. Grant, *Miracle and Natural Law in Graeco-Roman and Early Christian Thought*, 1952.
[13] *The City of God*, Book xxi, chapter 8 (Everyman's Edit., Vol. 2, p. 330).

it is not easy to answer. Matthew Arnold propounded the view that the study of the background of biblical miracles would be the end of them. He wrote: "Now from the moment this time commences, from the moment that the comparative history of all miracles is a conception entertained and a study admitted, the conclusion is certain, the reign of the Bible-miracles is doomed."[14] Since these words were written, the "comparative history of all miracles" has had constant attention in biblical scholarship; where, then, has it left Arnold's forecast? Does it now stand refuted, or confirmed, or perhaps just modified a little? Some would say refuted. With the rise of Barthianism and other variations of Neo-Calvinism a new conservatism has found favour amongst many biblical scholars, and its representatives would regard views like Matthew Arnold's as superficial and untrue. For example, C. E. B. Cranfield, after dividing the miracles into four classes—exorcisms, healing miracles, raisings of the dead, and nature miracles—remarks that "it does not seem unreasonable to believe that miracles of all four classes occurred".[15] Some stress the religious significance of the miracles, as well as its bearing on the question of their historicity. Alan Richardson, for instance, expresses the opinion that the gospel miracles embody religious truth which corroborates their historicity—at least, in substance if not in detail.[16] However, notable specialists exist who would express themselves very differently, being much less credulous concerning the historical reliability of these stories. Commonly, such scholars would be unwilling to accept the accounts of nature miracles and resuscitations of the dead as historical facts, though seeing no ground to deny that Jesus performed quite remarkable cures of some forms of disablement, illness, and mental disorder. But among sceptical and more credulous scholars alike, a fuller awareness is found to-day of the theological significance which all types of miracle had for Christians in the apostolic age, and for Jesus himself. Indeed, biblical scholarship has carried its investigation of the whole subject further and more deeply than had Matthew Arnold, and, on balance, even radical critics would tend to be more constructive than he, especially perhaps in expounding the religious significance of the miracles. With these observations,

[14] *God and the Bible*, Popular Edition, 1893, p. 19.
[15] *The Gospel according to St Mark* (in the Cambridge Greek Testament Commentary series), 1959, p. 86.
[16] See *The Miracle Stories of the Gospels*, 1941, p. 36 and also chapter vii.

Views Past and Present

however, we are approaching questions which come under examination in the next section.

2

Our review of what we have called the more negative aspects of the problem of the miracles has ended with remarks about the divergences of opinion which exist among the experts. Then what is the layman to think? In particular, what positive considerations emerge from specialist work to which attention should be given in making up one's mind concerning the trustworthiness of these stories? Let us now turn to this side of the question.

First of all, no good reason has appeared to doubt the personal integrity of the gospel writers. That they were men of their time must be assumed; and in their world even outstanding men of letters did not work to the methods and standards of historical accuracy expected of competent modern historians. But to accuse the gospel evangelists of indiscriminately submerging historical fact in a flood of miracle-mongering to serve the interests of theological propaganda would be outright injustice. They could, in fact, be remarkably objective in what they record. For example, the changes which are *not* made in order to bring the gospel traditions into conformity with the Christian beliefs and practices of the apostolic age are sometimes more surprising than those which are. In view of the background of apostolic thought about Jesus as the divine Son of God and heavenly Lord, how astonishing it is that St Mark's Gospel and St Luke's should keep the words, "Why callest thou me good? none is good save one, even God".[17] Another illustration of the same point occurs in St Matthew's and St Mark's accounts of the Last Supper. Neither evangelist includes the words, "This do in remembrance of me", notwithstanding the fact that they appear in St Paul's version of what Jesus said (1 Cor. 11. 23-5) — a report written before the gospels and one which represented the widespread practice of the church.[18] Certainly the faith of the apostolic

---

[17] Mark 10. 18; Luke 18. 19. The writer of St Matthew's Gospel evidently felt that this wording compromised the spiritual greatness of Jesus, since his version of the question reads, "Why askest thou me concerning that which is good?" (Matt. 19. 17).

[18] Luke 22. 19, of course, gives the words, "This do in remembrance of me"; but it is common knowledge that some early manuscripts of Luke omitted them; and whether the third evangelist did, or did not, write them is still a disputed question. Cf. this passage in the text of the *New English Bible*.

Christian community has left its stamp on what the gospels contain; but to overlook those passages which reveal predispositions to retain the traditional, even when current Christian usage was departing from it, is to see a distorted picture. The evangelists wrote to substantiate the Christian gospel as presented in their day; yet their interest in theology was infused with a concern for history. They meant to be honest recorders, as well as apologists and preachers; and the relative sobriety of their descriptions of the miracles is a further point in their favour, as more than one scholar has remarked.[19] And how free their narratives are—comparatively speaking—of extravagant and fanciful features is at once apparent when the canonical gospel miracles are compared with those in the apocryphal gospels, or in later Christian writers like Augustine and Bede, not to mention the fantastic wonder-tales which circulated in the medieval Church.

The next point concerns the primitiveness of the tradition which reports miracles performed by Jesus. How early were these stories in existence? Are they an original element of the narrative tradition now embodied in our gospels? The answer is not in doubt. Detailed analysis of the oral and literary stages through which the contents of the gospels passed before reaching their present written form has now been in progress for more than a century, but no scholar would claim to have unearthed an early layer of narrative traditions which contained no miracles or allusions to miracles. And that, from the first, Christians did in fact tell of miracles which their Lord worked is further confirmed by an examination of the earliest Christian preaching. They witnessed to a Christ "who went about doing good and healing all that were oppressed of the devil".[20] Research on the sayings tradition has yielded similar results. Some of its most primitive elements reveal Jesus himself making reference to his miracles, as in the Q passage in which he refers the messengers from John

[19] E.g. M. Goguel, *Life of Jesus*, English trans., 1933, p. 218; J. S. Lawton, *Miracles and Revelation*, 1959, p. 155. That the gospel writers were strongly motivated by historical interests, alongside theological and liturgical ones, is beginning to find renewed emphasis in New Testament study. Cf. C. F. D. Moule, "The Intention of the Evangelists", an essay in *New Testament Essays*, 1959, pp. 165-79; H. Riesenfeld, *The Gospel Tradition and its Beginnings*, 1957.

[20] Acts 10. 38. Cf. Acts 2. 22. C. H. Dodd has expressed the view that Rom. 15. 18-19 implies that Paul knew of the miracles attributed to Jesus—see *The Bible Today*, 1946, chapter 4. Compare also the rendering of Rom. 15. 18-19 in the R.V. margin.

the Baptist to the fact that "the blind receive their sight, and the lame walk, the lepers are cleansed, and the deaf hear, and the dead are raised up, and the poor have good tidings preached to them".[21] Thus on the evidence of the earliest reports of both his deeds and his words, the Jesus of the gospels wrought miracles.

But how far do these arguments really carry us? In spite of them, the miracle-stories seem to contain so much that remains incredible to modern man. To be sure; yet, in acknowledging this, another point calls for repeated emphasis: whilst the difficulties of the miracles readily obtrude themselves, let not the possibilities be overlooked, or underestimated! They often are. Rufus M. Jones remarked: "There seem to be almost no limits to the curative effects of suggestive faith and emotional expectation. The shrines at Lourdes in France and at Saint Ann's in Quebec have furnished vivid demonstration of this principle."[22] This statement may be incautiously worded, but in principle it is true enough. It comes to this: where unusual religious activities are concerned, ordinary experience can too easily be made normative. That he was attaching too much finality to normal human experience was one of the criticisms which T. H. Huxley brought to bear upon Hume's treatment of miracles, even though Huxley shared Hume's sceptical conclusions.[23] This kind of caution is particularly apt when it is a question of estimating the capacities of outstanding religious personalities, and for the obvious reason that religiously most of us live on mediocre levels. We are spiritual pygmies alongside Jesus, unfamiliar with the heights and depths of his life with God. What, then, do we think to be our qualifications for assessing his powers? New Testament miracles and many subsequent Christian miracles emerged, as William Sanday and John Henry Newman rightly observed, from a background of faith and prayer. To undertake analysis of what is possible to faith and prayer is in all conscience bold; when it concerns the faith and prayer of Jesus, it may easily become presumptuous. From the standpoint of this consideration, Sanday again helps—at least with some of the miracle stories. He wrote; "Deduct something perhaps from the historical statement of

21 Matt. 11. 5 (Luke 7. 22). Cf. Matt. 12. 28 (Luke 11. 20); 11. 21 (Luke 10. 13); Luke 4. 16-30; etc.
22 From the Foreword to H. J. Cadbury's edition of George Fox's 'Book of Miracles', 1948, p. xii.
23 T. H. Huxley, Collected Essays, Vol. vi, 1894, pp. 154-8.

the fact; and add something to our conception of what is possible . . . and if the two ends do not exactly meet, we may yet see that they are not very far from meeting."[24]

Let us now turn to a question which has been much to the fore in more recent scholarly work. It is that of the religious meaning and value of Christ's miracles. What interpretation did Jesus himself give them? How do the gospel writers use them? Even if the historical trustworthiness of the miracle-narratives could be assumed, would they add anything religiously significant to our understanding of Jesus and the Christian gospel for our own day and generation?

A careful look at Christ's own attitude to his achievements reveals that he did not use his capacity to work miracles mainly in order to establish a claim to be the messianic Son of God, or with the object of winning a following by spectacular demonstration of unique powers. It is true that the Fourth Gospel sometimes pictures him acting thus: it represents his miracles as "signs" by which "he manifested his glory" that men might believe on him.[25] The first three gospels also show traces of the same conception of the Lord's behaviour. But the weight of the evidence is against it. Jesus' personal attitude is probably more truly reflected in the description of his temptation in the wilderness, which seems to imply a repudiation of the use of divine powers in order to impress others, or in some of those passages, found especially in Mark, speaking of secrecy imposed upon those whom he healed. In Mark 8. 12, again, we have the very forthright statement that "There shall no sign be given unto this generation". Thus when Christians use the miracle-narratives to demonstrate Christ's Lordship, they take an apologetic line which he himself shunned. Yet certainly Jesus believed that his unusual powers over mental disorder and other types of illness provided further confirmation of the operation of a special measure of the Spirit of God in and through his life. They were a sign that in his mission God was putting forth his mighty arm to renew every aspect of the life of man and nature which had been broken, corrupted, or enslaved in bondage to sin and Satan. No less was the range of divine redemption; and inasmuch as the miracles helped to illustrate it, they were

[24] *Life of Christ in Recent Research*, 1907, p. 223. Chapter 8 on "Miracles" in this book is still valuable.   [25] Cf. John 2. 11; 20. 30f; etc.

an integral part of Christ's gospel. "If I by the Spirit of God cast out devils," he said, "then is the kingdom of God come upon you" (Matt. 12. 28).

If such was Jesus' view, what conceptions of the miracles are to be attributed to the evangelists? How far do they share his thought, and how far do they differ? As has already been indicated, they were more ready than Jesus was to use the miracles as explicit evidence that he was indeed the Christ, the Son of God; and that the miracles illustrated the arrival and the scope of God's salvation was an idea which they too adopted — in fact, they amplified it. Since they probably accepted as historical all the miracle-stories which they used, they had a wide and varied range of material with which to do this. For them, indeed, the different kinds of miracles were acted parables, having their special messages, just as truly as the Lord's spoken parables. This is the viewpoint behind the difficult words of Mark 4. 11f: "Unto them that are without, all things *are done* [or, "all things *happen*"] in parables: that seeing they may see, and not perceive; and hearing they may hear, and not understand." Obviously the passage refers to actions (things seen), as well as to words (things heard); all are equally "parables", and, moreover, parables to the religious meaning of which unbelievers were blind. How much of the wording of this quotation derives from Jesus is a disputed question, but it certainly represents Mark's viewpoint and that of his circle. It is not surprising, therefore, that in secondary and interpretative parts of the gospels suggestions that the miracles have symbolical significance occur, and even explicit developments of the spiritual truths which they were held to symbolize. Mark 8. 17-21 almost certainly implies the presence of some hidden religious meaning in the miraculous feedings of the five thousand and the four thousand — a meaning which even the disciples had failed to see. In John 6, the feeding of the five thousand receives a quite definite religious interpretation: it was a revelation of the truth that Jesus feeds men with the bread of life from heaven, and is himself the bread. In the same gospel, the calling forth of Lazarus from the tomb signifies that Jesus is the resurrection and the life. Sometimes, however, it is only the context in which an evangelist relates a miracle which hints that he attaches a symbolical sense to it. Thus Mark may well have understood the withering of the fig tree as a miracle which foreshadowed

God's judgement on Jerusalem or Israel: Israel had failed to be God's life-giving tree for the nations, and would henceforth be supplanted by the more fruitful vine of the Christian Church.[26]

It is not difficult to see that, handled in such ways, the miracles could retain a place in the witness of the early Church as a fully integrated part of the gospel. They were certainly that to the writer of John 20. 30f. They did not embarrass. Far from it: they were cogent manifestations of the truth. They confirmed the faith that the Spirit of the Lord was upon Jesus, anointing him "to preach good tidings to the poor . . . to proclaim release to the captives, and recovering of sight to the blind, to set at liberty them that are bruised, to proclaim the acceptable year of the Lord" (Luke 4. 18f).

Can the gospel miracles provide any such victory song for us to-day? Do they stand near enough to historical reality for this? For any writer to suppose himself qualified to give thoughtful people the definitive answer, would be presumptuous. Ultimately, every reader must form his own views about the worth of the miracle-stories, and should be encouraged to do so, as honestly as he can. God expects no more of him—and, to be sure, no less! But something further should perhaps be said about the Christian attitude to the problems they raise. Broadly speaking, there are two avenues of approach: the one of scrupulous historical research, and the other that of faith.

The foregoing essay has dealt mostly with the way of historical research, which has been seen to lead to results partly negative, sometimes inconclusive, yet in a measure corroborative. But perhaps the Christian can come yet nearer to the truth by means of the more specifically religious approach of faith?

In Professor Alan Richardson's book, *The Miracle Stories of the Gospels*, it is stated that final judgement on the historicity of these stories and their present-day religious value must be left to faith. Whilst the "exercise of our critical and historical faculties in respect of the detail of each particular miracle" (pp. 128f) is

[26] There must, of course, be caution and restraint in estimating the extent to which the gospel writers saw symbolical meanings in the miracles. M. Werner in *Der Einfluss paulinischer Theologie im Markusevangelium*, 1923, saw symbolical uses of narratives nowhere in Mark. G. Volkmar saw it everywhere—see his *Marcus und die Synopse der Evangelien*, 1876. The former seems as definitely in error as the latter. In the nineteenth century, much use was made of the symbolical exposition of the miracles by British scholars like B. F. Westcott and R. C. Trench.

commended, in the last resort, we are told, "the answer to the question, Did the miracles happen? is always a personal answer ... It is the 'Yes' of faith to the challenge which confronts us in the New Testament presentation of Christ—the only Christ we can know" (p. 127). Many theologians write like this to-day. Often, however, it is difficult to see where these writers (and the book just quoted is no exception) draw the line between what on the one hand genuine knowledge and reason prescribe and what on the other hand faith should endorse, or even by what means the line is drawn. Who or what decides at what point "our critical and historical faculties" must give way and faith take over? Is it, in fact, unfair to say that in practice the manner in which this problem is solved is too often quite individualistic, and indeed, even arbitrary and obscurantist?

Austin Farrer's criticism of R. Bultmann in the last chapter of *Kerygma and Myth* [27] provides a suitable concrete case for closer examination of the faith approach. Speaking of what he describes as "the virginal conception of our Saviour in Mary's womb", Farrer takes Bultmann to task because, in Farrer's words, "Bultmann appears to beg the question. He writes as though he knew that God never bends physical fact into special conformity with divine intention ... Bultmann seems to be convinced that he knows this, but I am not convinced that I know it" (p. 216). Subsequently, however, Farrer speaks of "what Christians find in Christ through faith" (p. 220) and of "the use of faith to confirm evidence" (pp. 220f) about miracles, including miraculous events like the virgin birth and the corporeal resurrection of Jesus Christ. "Thus it is possible", he writes, "through faith and evidence together, and through neither alone, to believe that Christ really and corporeally rose from the dead" (p. 220). In fact, Austin Farrer, like Alan Richardson, seems to claim that faith can finally settle the question of the historicity of this or that miracle and does so affirmatively in most instances. Hence the phrase "the use of faith to confirm evidence" is apparently meant quite literally. But if, as he contends, Bultmann is begging the question concerning the historicity of the miracle-stories by attaching too much finality to modern scientific knowledge, is not Farrer begging the question by attaching too much finality to the function of faith? For how can faith confirm

[27] Edited by H.-W. Bartsch; Eng. trans. by R. H. Fuller, S.P.C.K., 1960.

what honest, historical research by men of faith has left doubtful? What would be the nature of a faith to which one could attribute a cognitive capacity so far-reaching and ultimate?

By "faith", Farrer does not intend to mean immature credulity, an arbitrary determination to believe, irrespective of the nature of the evidence. Far from it. The faith to which he refers consists in the two elements of trusting, personal commitment to Jesus Christ as Lord and the willingness to believe extraordinary things about him which arises from fuller discovery of Christ's greatness, consequent upon personal surrender to him. Both aspects of faith appear in the statement, "What Christians find in Christ through faith inclines them at certain points to accept with regard to him testimony about matter of fact which would be inconclusive if offered with regard to any other man" (p. 220).

But does this clarification of the sense in which Farrer speaks of faith help to substantiate the claim for "the use of faith to confirm evidence" when investigating the historical truth of the gospel accounts of miracles? How can an attitude of personal trust, or a willingness to believe that Jesus had exceptional powers, ever establish with certainty some unusual occurrence told of his past life? Such a trust in a person, however implicit, such a willingness to believe, however ready, give direct access only to the nature of his personality, not to any specific action associated with him in his past. The most, therefore, that such faith in Christ can do is to raise the degree of probability which we may rightly attach to this or that extraordinary story about him. Our increased knowledge of his greatness, derived from our experience of him, allows us to say, even in the presence of inconclusive historical evidence, that a certain otherwise incredible story may *possibly* be correct. From that point, we may then feel justified in moving further to declare, "I believe this". But that is not faith confirming evidence, but faith bringing about a jump beyond evidence; and small though the jump may seem, conclusive proof is still lacking that we have come down on something true. We should be quite frank about this qualification of the finality of the faith approach.

But looking at the gospel miracles in the attitude of faith, how wide is the jump between evidence and belief over which faith must be able to carry us? To express it more literally, even when faith does all it can, how considerable is the residue of unknowable or uncertain elements in the problem? And of what nature are they? These questions bring us to one of the greater difficulties about the faith approach.

Faith might carry us a longer way towards confirming the evidence for specific gospel miracles, if the evidence to be confirmed were evidence given directly by Jesus himself, of whose personality faith helps us to learn so much. As through faith in him, knowledge of his outstanding trustworthiness and potentialities grew, claims which he made for himself, even if first thought unbelievable, might then in truth become unquestionable. But we have no such evidence: the miracle narratives in the gospels come to us in writing, not direct from Jesus himself but in secondary sources compiled by others. If, therefore, faith is to substantiate this evidence, it must reveal and confirm not only the powers of Jesus, but also the reliability of the recorders of his work—the gospel evangelists and those who had care of the gospel traditions before their commitment to writing. Faith must be able to assure us that these men never reported what Jesus did not experience or perform. That is, the gap of the unknown to be crossed before a decision to believe can be reached extends not only from the gospel evidence to Jesus, as it were, but further—over the longer distance from the evidence to Jesus *and to them*! Can, then, faith ever hope to enable us to cross that stretch, and find these recorders reliable with certainty, especially when careful historical research discloses that, although they were honest men to the best of their ability, they were subject to human fallibility? The difficulty is that faith in Christ and the resultant personal experience of him can tell us nothing, or not much, about the personalities of the individuals who preserved the gospel traditions and the evangelists who compiled the gospels. Nor have we adequate access to them by other means. Most of them, for one thing, are entirely unknown to us. These points set limits to the use of faith as a means of substantiating the gospel miracle-stories which writers like Austin Farrer and Alan Richardson appear to overlook. It therefore seems necessary to conclude that to speak of "the use of faith to confirm evidence" when we are examining gospel accounts of miraculous events is an over-statement which obscures the measure of some of the relevant problems. The Christian who considers it essential to face these fully, must therefore be content to say that however many of the miracles become entirely credible to him as a result of faith in Jesus Christ, faith does not, and cannot, remove the doubtfulness attaching to others as a result of historical research. It will, moreover, be inevitable that assessments of the extent of such uncertainty will vary from person to person, and this inevitability should be freely acknowledged in all Christian apologetic treating of the miracles.[28]

None the less, and despite its limitations, the faith attitude is a basic need alongside informed, thoughtful study of Jesus and biblical revelation. A teacher of mine used to remark on the way in which some people dismissed the poetry of Browning as hopelessly obscure, forgetting how much they thereby disclosed their own inadequacies. "Beyond a certain point," he would say, "you don't judge Browning: he judges you." The faith approach to the Bible is for one thing a recognition that here, too, the same happens; and faith is a willingness that it shall happen. So faith involves repentant readiness to be judged by biblical revelation, in the very act of offering judgement upon it. Faith is thus eagerness to have one's eyes opened to the heights of spiritual achievement described in the Bible; and it fulfils itself in personal response to God, in the whole-hearted self-surrender to his will which proceeds from the con-

[28] A valuable and discriminating treatment of the miracles published since the writing of my essay is the book by Professor R. H. Fuller, entitled *Interpreting the Miracles* (S.C.M. Press, 1963). Professor Fuller also emphasizes the importance of the faith approach, if one is to recognize miracle stories as accounts of extraordinary interventions of God in history. But here again the plea shrouds Fuller's final position in some obscurity. By means of critical analysis, he decides that it is improbable that Jesus resuscitated dead men or performed the nature miracles, and that only the reports of healings and exorcisms are trustworthy—though "we can never be certain of the authenticity of any actual miracle story in the gospels .... most of them have probably been shaped out of generalized memories" (p. 39). In the final count, however, he makes an attempt to show how in and by means of the faith attitude one can come to see all the gospel miracles, nature and healing, as narratives which "proclaim to us a God of miracles, a God who acts, who intervenes and interferes in specific events" (p. 122). In propounding this view, the question whether the miracles happened or not is even played down as "really neither here nor there" (p. 122). But is not this astonishing, since what God *actually does or does not do* in the form of special interventions in human situations is the very point at issue? Only if a miracle occurred, only if it *was* an act, can it convincingly demonstrate "a God who acts, who intervenes and interferes in specific events" in the manner described in any one miracle story. This further implies that "miracles" which can be shown to have happened must stand in quite a different category as revelations of the true nature of the "God of miracles" from those that have little or no historical basis.

viction that the spiritual discoveries to which Christ leads occur only at the level of the personal commitment for which Christ asks. Will such a faith radically change our understanding of the gospel miracles? J. S. Lawton suggests that it will. To men of knowledge, tempered with faith, "miracle", he maintains, "has actually moved from the circumference to the very centre of revelation".[29] That may not, however, be the experience of all men of knowledge and faith. They need not be disturbed thereby. Faith, as we have seen, cannot settle all the problems which the miracles present; and for many it certainly does not lead to the conviction that they happened just as recorded. Faith, to be sure, may be truly of the persuasion that Jesus is a greater Jesus, if they *did not* all happen just as recorded.

None the less, no great religious insight is reached, nor great religious accomplishment, save for the faith which is not earth-bound, nor held down to mediocre levels of expectation set by human knowledge and judgement. There must be the faith which removes mountains: faith which comes from God, to set forth the nature of the world and the scope of Christ's redemption in the light of what God is and God's spirit can do. In this light, extended vision arises of the range of our Lord's mighty works; and out of it will issue a wider appreciation of the gospel miracles as illustrations of the senses in which he came to seek and to save those who are lost. God through Christ still does such things as are recorded in the miracle-narratives—to some extent literally; but if not literally, then metaphorically in the sense that he binds up broken lives, frees men from captivity to their fears and sin, feeds those who hunger and thirst after righteousness, speaks peace amidst the tempests of anger which shake the nations, so that even on earth we may behold something of the blessedness of the Kingdom of Heaven. Than such as these, there are no greater miracles. They also mean that it is true that when our own attitude is right, God "is able to do exceeding abundantly above all that we ask or think". This reconsideration of the miracles described in the gospels may therefore fittingly end with the words which Jesus uttered after one of the most puzzling of them: "Have faith in God" (Mark 11. 22).

[29] *Miracles and Revelation*, p. 254.

© G. H. Boobyer, 1964.

3

HEALING IN THE NEW TESTAMENT[1]

F. N. DAVEY

TO MOST people the acts of healing attributed to Jesus appear to form a separate class among the actions we call his miracles. We make this distinction whether we accept the traditional view that these were exceptional acts of supernatural power, or whether we incline to rationalize them, emphasizing the elements of faith in the recipient or in those who brought him to Jesus, and regarding them as in some sense natural events in a world in which spirit in the last resort triumphs over flesh and mind over matter. But, to judge from the New Testament, neither acts of healing, nor the whole range of "mighty works", were isolated in the mind of Christ, or in the minds of the evangelists, or in the minds of the apostles. For all of them, the material of the Gospel is one. The acts of healing are set firmly in the context of the whole ministry of Jesus, and of the whole life and faith of the early Church. Studied in that context, we find in them precisely the same pattern as is discernible in Christ's sayings, his parables, his discourses, his calling of his disciples, his controversies with those who withstood him—indeed, in the whole course of his ministry, from Galilee to Calvary. This pattern we shall also find reflected in the outlook of the primitive Church, though (as is usual in reflections) reversed.

[1] The substance of the first of four Lectures on Healing, by different lecturers, given at St Mark's, Hamilton Terrace.

Healing in the New Testament   51

I

In what we believe to be the earliest complete Gospel, the Gospel of Mark, we find details that suggest that Jesus healed as any contemporary wonder-worker might heal. He is said to have used saliva to anoint the tongue of a stammerer and the eyes of a blind man, as others in the ancient world are said to have done. He is said to have taken sick people by the hand, or touched them; or to have healed them by contact when they touched the fringe of his garment; and to this also there are other ancient parallels. He is said to have used commands that seemed to be "a common form for binding a person by the means of a spell, so as to make him powerless for harm, and to have inquired the name of the supposed devil" which, as we know from documents of the same epoch was thought to be a means of exerting control over it. Moreover, Jesus himself appears to have assumed that in healing and exorcising he was not unique. When accused of exorcising by the power of Beelzeboul, he is said to have answered (not in Mark, but in the source which Matthew perhaps shared with Luke): "If I by Beelzeboul cast out devils, by whom do your sons cast them out?" (Luke 11. 19; Matt. 12. 27). Jesus does not seem to have regarded the mere fact that he healed and exorcized as in any way exceptional. In some centres of Greek civilization medical science was already in its infancy, and where Judaism met the cultured Greek world the profession of physician was already becoming recognized as a gift of God, to be used with confidence (e.g. Eccl. 38. 1-15). But Jesus appears, without hesitation, to use the more primitive methods of that part of the world in which he had grown up. It would be very dangerous to read more than that into these fragmentary, though primitive, records of his use of material means and outward signs.

Moreover, the acts of healing ascribed to Jesus are often works of compassion. He is moved to heal or to exorcize by evident physical or mental distress, which he takes very seriously indeed. But this is not always the case. Sometimes there is no mention of compassion. Once (if we follow a famous variant reading) he is said to have been moved not by compassion but by anger, and to have spoken with indignation to the man he had just healed of leprosy. Perhaps he acted not merely from compassion for distress, but out of fury at the powers of evil which confronted him (Mark 1. 41, 43). He exorcizes a man with an unclean spirit, in the synagogue at Capernaum, and another in the country of the Gerasenes, although both these possessed men approach him in a hostile manner. Again, though not always, some suggestion of faith may seem to enter in: faith on the part of the recipient himself, as in the case of Bar Timaeus, who goes on crying out "Jesus, thou son of David, have mercy upon me" although many tell him to be quiet (Mark 10. 52); or of the woman who touches his robe (Mark 5. 34); or, more often perhaps, faith on the part of those who bring the sick and infirm to him, or who speak to him about them, like the father of the epileptic boy (Mark 9. 23, 24), the Syrophoenician woman (Mark 7. 29), or the ruler of the synagogue whose daughter was accounted dead (Mark 5. 36).

So far we might be tempted to portray Jesus as using, simply and confidently, the methods of his locality and time, out of compassion at evident distress, out of anger at the evident spectacle of the ravages wrought by the powers of evil, and in response to some kind of evident confidence in his powers, on someone else's part. All these factors must be kept in mind, for they are significant. But, as we look further, we find that the total picture is not so simple.

The morning after he had healed many that were sick with divers diseases, and cast out many devils, when all men were seeking him, he went out alone to pray in a solitary place. "And when his disciples came to fetch him, he said: Let us go elsewhere into the next towns, that I may preach there also; for to this end came I forth. And he went into their synagogues throughout all Galilee, preaching and casting out devils" (Mark 1. 38, 39). If his acts of healing meant no more than that it was important that he should heal, out of compassion for suffering and distress at the power of evil, wherever there was some glimmering of faith, then—the more he healed, the more he would have accomplished. But the significance of his healing acts is not merely *quantitative*, to perform as many cures as possible. He has no hesitation in leaving those who are thronging to him in faith. It must therefore have been, partly at least, *qualitative*, as necessarily accompanying his preaching, and perhaps as demonstrating its meaning.

Indeed, the healing acts of Jesus are linked intimately with his

Healing in the New Testament 53

Word. Those who hear him at Capernaum, at the beginning of his ministry, comment with amazement: "What is this? a new teaching! with authority he commandeth even the unclean spirits, and they obey him" (Mark 1. 27). While he is speaking the Word to the crowd in the house at Capernaum a paralytic is brought to him, and he makes the command to take up his bed and walk—that is, physical healing—the sign of spiritual healing: "that ye may know that the Son of man hath power on earth to forgive sins" (Mark 2. 10)—forgiveness being, of course, the prerogative of God. In the next incident recorded by Mark this movement from the outward work to the invisible salvation of God is even more clearly emphasized. Jesus sits down to eat with publicans and sinners because "they that are whole have no need of a physician, but they that are sick: I came not to call the righteous, but sinners" (Mark 2. 17).

In those parts of their Gospels which Matthew and Luke have in common, but which are not found in Mark, we notice that it is when the crowd is thronging him because of his healing power that he speaks the Beatitudes—proclaiming to those preoccupied with physical need God's coming, final, satisfaction of their entire neediness before him (cf. Matt. 4. 23—5. 12 with Luke 6. 17-26). In the same way, in Mark's Gospel, the stilling of the storm runs on to the healing of the storm in the demoniac's heart (Mark 4. 35—5. 20); while the feeding of the 5,000 and of the 4,000 (acts also called out by compassion at evident physical distress) find their full significance in the warning to "beware of the leaven of Herod". The crucial human distress is sin in the human heart. To Jesus, it appears, there is no line of demarcation, even in thought, between his compassionate acts and his Gospel. Moreover, while his visible, compassionate acts, in the physical or mental spheres, are of real importance in themselves, they are even more important because they bear witness to, and demonstrate, what is a matter between God and the souls of men—the ultimate distress of human sin; the gift of the ultimate salvation of God.

There are other pointers in this direction. For instance, on at least two occasions in Mark's Gospel Jesus performed miracles with great circumspectness, taking the sick man away from the crowd, out of the village, and healing him in the presence of the disciples only (Mark 7. 33; 8. 23). So, when he restored the ruler of the synagogue's daughter to life, he took only Peter and James and John with him (Mark 5. 37). These, it would appear, were acts that must be seen by those who would subsequently bear witness.

Luke alone records the remark, after an act of healing: "Ought not this woman, being a daughter of Abraham, whom Satan had bound, lo, these eighteen years, to have been loosed from this bond on the day of the sabbath?" (Luke 13. 16). The issue is more than humanitarian. The pharisees might well have answered that if the woman had waited eighteen years it would not matter if she waited a few hours longer. But Jesus, perhaps like others of his time, seems to have expected that because the sabbath is the day of the Lord, the coming of the salvation of God would usher in an eternal sabbath. The Christ *must* do these things on the sabbath because the sabbath above all days points to the true significance of what he is doing.

Again, when Jesus healed a leper, he sent him to show himself to the priest, offering for his cleansing the things which Moses commanded, "for a testimony unto them" (Mark 1. 44). Of course, it was the priest's business to see that one who had been a leper was really healed, and to admit him back into the society from which he had been excluded. But is that all that the phrase implies? It crops up in other connections — to the disciples: "Whatsoever place shall not receive you, and they hear you not, as ye go forth thence, shake off the dust that is under your feet for a testimony against them" (Mark 6. 11); to the disciples again: "Before governors and kings shall ye stand for my sake, for a testimony unto them" (Mark 13. 9). We may recall how Jesus answers John Baptist's messengers, according to Matthew and Luke: "Tell John what things ye have seen and heard; the blind receive their sight, the lame walk, the lepers are cleansed, and the deaf hear, the dead are raised up, the poor have good tidings preached to them. And blessed is he, whosoever shall find none occasion of stumbling in me" (Matt. 11. 4-6; Luke 7. 22, 23).

The answer given to John Baptist is for the most part couched in phrases taken from Isaiah — phrases declaring what would happen when God acted and brought redemption, salvation, to Israel (Isa. 29. 18; 35. 5, 6). In Luke's account of our Lord's first preachings in the synagogue at Nazareth, his own home town, Jesus also quotes similar passages of Isaiah (Isa. 61. 1, 2; 58. 6) and

Healing in the New Testament

goes on to say: "To-day hath this scripture been fulfilled in your ears" (Luke 4. 16-30). At this, his fellow townsmen certainly find occasion of stumbling in him. By setting his Gospel in the context of the expectation concerning the coming of God's Kingdom, the messianic age, by presenting all he said and did as the fulfilment of the whole great hope of Israel, Jesus in effect makes a claim so tremendous that those who believe themselves the people of God are offended. They cannot see, as Matthew saw when he recounted how Jesus cast out the spirits with a word and healed all that were sick, that this was the fulfilment of that which was "spoken by Isaiah the prophet, saying, Himself took our infirmities, and bare our diseases" (Matt. 8. 17).

It has been traditional among Christians to think of Christ's miracles as proofs of his divine powers, to think of his detailed fulfilment of certain prophecies as justifying our claim that he is the Christ. There may well be truth in both these statements; yet to make them, just like that, is not to be true to these earliest records of his ministry. He does not claim that his acts of healing prove supernatural powers—others do similar acts. He does not say, even, "You must regard what I am doing as authoritative because it tallies with what Isaiah has lead us to expect the Messiah to do". What he says is, "If I by the finger (spirit) of God cast out devils, then is the Kingdom of God come upon you" (Luke 11. 20; Matt. 12. 28). "Blessed are the eyes which see the things that ye see: for I say unto you, that many prophets and kings desired to see the things which ye see, and saw them not; and to hear the things which ye hear, and heard them not" (Luke 10. 23, 24). Jesus is concerned with the whole, universal, redemptive work of God, which he knows, with his own coming, to be upon men, at their very doors, in their very midst. Details are important, such details as healings and exorcisms, but not as suggesting that God has now for the first time vouchsafed certain powers to men, to add to their armoury for alleviating suffering, first through Jesus himself and afterwards through his Church. They are important, because these fragmentary acts and partially understood words—and we might add, all the natural phenomena and incidents which to Jesus seem luminous with witness to the Kingdom of God—can, by God's spirit and grace, open men's eyes to the fact that God's ultimate salvation confronts them now. The theme, not of certain passages of Isaiah merely, nor yet of a few of the great psalms alone, but of the whole Old Testament, is laid upon Jesus—if only God's people can perceive it and receive it. God's forgiveness, his remission, is being offered to men. The bonds of wickedness are being loosed by Jesus. He is offering liberty to the captives. He is beseeching the wicked to forsake their way, to return to God and live. For him the world, both visible and invisible, is one. Men are in the universal grip of sin. Of sin, sickness is a visible symptom and demonstration. Men are being ravaged by the powers of evil ranged against the power of Almighty God. Of this, too, possession is a recognizable symptom and demonstration. From the moment Jesus goes forth in the power of the spirit, his ministry is a symptom and demonstration of the kingdom and power of God, binding evil, loosing the prisoners, healing the sick, raising up those who are dying in sin, because the acceptable year of the Lord—or, if you like, the great sabbath of God (any metaphor may help men to see)—is come. This is not understood as Christ's disclosure of latent supernatural powers that have always been accessible to men, although hitherto unknown to them, but as the breaking into the order of this world, from outside, of one stronger than the powers of evil (cf. Mark 3. 27, etc.).

But—and this was foreshadowed when they took up stones to cast at him at Nazareth—men persist in seeing all these symptoms, these demonstrations, as things in themselves. Gifts of God they may be, but none the less gifts to be snatched at for their intrinsic value in time and space, and for nothing else. Those who throng him with their sick at one moment, find occasion of stumbling in him the next. "He could do no mighty work there" (in Nazareth, for instance, as it happens, but it was true of Jerusalem also) "save that he laid his hands upon a few sick folk, and healed them. And he marvelled because of their unbelief" (Mark 6. 5, 6). Unbelief could not stop his alleviation of distress, for this was not faith-healing. But unbelief could obstruct the Gospel of the salvation of God. That, and nothing else but that, was the mighty work which he desired to accomplish in Nazareth, and throughout Galilee and Judaea and the whole world.

As the ministry of Jesus proceeds, the works of compassion cease, the proclamation of the Gospel changes to controversy and refutation. He begins to set his face to go up to Jerusalem, and to speak to his disciples about his suffering, rejection, and death. Those who should have learned from the teaching, the parables, the words of Jesus, and from his acts of compassion and healing, that the redemption of God has drawn near bringing salvation from sin and death, have evaluated all these things in terms only of time and space. It is at this point that Jesus gives Bartimaeus his sight—a welcome reminder to the reader that even the blindness of his disciples will eventually be removed (Mark 10. 46-52). For even those healed have not understood him or his actions. Peter has rebuked him. Presently, all are to foresake him and flee. But it is when Jesus himself, loaded with the sins that are not his, with all the sin of the world, is brought down into the dust of death, that those who still love him, even though they have not understood him are shown him risen from the dead, and begin to see that here, in Christ crucified and risen, is the place of understanding, the fulfilment, the meaning, of all that he had said and done in his ministry on earth. Here, in this particular moment in time and space, the whole, eternal salvation of God is made accessible to men and women. As we are told in the Gospel of St John, "The Son of man must be lifted up; that whosoever believeth may in him have eternal life. For God so loved the world, that he gave his only begotten Son, that whosoever believeth on him should not perish, but have eternal life" (John 3. 14-16).

2

The longer ending attached later to the Gospel of Mark concludes with these words: "They went forth, and preached everywhere, the Lord working with them, and confirming the word by the signs that followed" (Mark 16. 20). This brief sentence sums up the healing and exorcizing ministry of the apostles and the early Church, and sets it in its right perspective. The pattern of words and works discernible in our Lord's ministry is reflected, but reversed, in the primitive Church. Jesus had tried to open men's eyes to the imminence, in himself, in his coming, of the ultimate salvation of God, by trying to make them see the true meaning of —among other things—the very real works of mercy which he wrought. Men saw only his works. They could not perceive his witness to the salvation of God. But, with the sight of his resurrection from the death of the cross, his disciples have been given the understanding of the Holy Spirit (the fourth Gospel affirms this insistently). They have apprehended all this, not as men, but with, as it were, the eyes and mind of God. This becomes their theme — the ultimate salvation of God, wrought and revealed through Jesus Christ crucified and risen. It forms the beginning and end of their thought. It is the subject of their preaching, the controlling motive of their life, the key to their whole calling and their entire world. And now the works of healing take their proper place in their Gospel; not, as in the Galilean ministry of Jesus, as actions which may draw men's eyes towards God's invisible salvation, but as actions which, for those who are entirely obsessed with God's salvation and created by it, follow naturally from it.

3

Such works of mercy, wrought in the name of Christ, we read of in the Acts of the Apostles, and assume from certain references in the Epistles; but they were only on the periphery of the apostolic Gospel — "signs that followed". It is evident from the fourth Gospel that some misunderstood them, and in spite of their supposed belief in Christ tried to bring them into the centre of the Gospels, as though a new order had entered the world, in which God offers men certain dependable, this-worldly blessings.

In the fourth Gospel the mighty works of Jesus are called "signs". This is not because they have in themselves any less reality. They are real works of mercy; they satisfy those in real distress. But the evangelist appears to choose the word "signs" because he wants it to be clear that their significance lies outside what they actually achieve in time and space.

Secondly, the synoptic picture of the crowds thronging Jesus with their sick is repeated, but criticized. For instance, "when he was in Jerusalem at the passover, during the feast, many believed on his Name, beholding his signs which he did. But Jesus did not trust himself to them, for that he knew all men" (John 2. 23, 24). Thus is the scene set for his conversation with Nicodemus (John 3. 1-21), who, because of these signs, is quite sure that Jesus is a teacher come from God. But Jesus, who is being presented as very much more than that, knows that "faith which moves from and towards physical healing cannot be trusted".[2] Nicodemus, a trained theologian, has no inkling of what Jesus is talking about when he speaks of the invisible Kingdom of God and the new birth from above by water and the Spirit—the real theme even of these outward signs. And so the conversation ends with the prediction of Jesus's death on the cross, of his resurrection from the dead, and of God's ultimate judgement of men on the basis of belief on the Name of his only begotten Son. Nicodemus, like those who sought nothing from Jesus but healing, had come by night, in darkness. For such, there is no light, no place of understanding, except the cross and the light by which it is glorified. Yet—and this is most important—physical healing *is itself*, even in this Gospel— perhaps above all in this Gospel—a parable; and the confidence it evokes, though not itself faith, "produces a situation eloquent of faith".

Thirdly, there are other possible misunderstandings of the works of Jesus. These are carefully guarded against in the fourth Gospel's accounts of the Healing of the Nobleman's Son, and the Healing of the Cripple at Bethesda (John 4. 46—5. 47), where it is made clear not only that miracles of healing are not the goal of faith, but that they are not means by which Jesus sought to exalt himself. Here, as in the synoptic Gospels, these miracles of healing are set in the midst of teaching, and are an integral part of the Word of God. More clearly than in the synoptic Gospels—though, as we have seen, it *should* have been quite clear there—our Lord's whole thought and theme lie *even beyond himself*. He has come to glorify the Father, to reveal the Father's invisible nature, to accomplish the Father's eternal work. Yet, what Jesus says and does in time and space is an integral part of this work of God. "My Father worketh until now, and I work" (John 5. 17). Faith is no faith, if it stops short even at faith in Jesus in time and space. Faith begins to be faith when the Father is honoured in the honouring of the Son whom the Father has sent. Here again the thought moves on irresistibly to the death and resurrection of Jesus, where alone full understanding is to be found. "Verily, verily, I say unto you, he that heareth my word, and believeth him that sent me, hath eternal life, and cometh not into judgement, but hath passed out of

[2] This, and the two quotations that follow, are from Hoskyns: *The Fourth Gospel.*

death into life. Verily, verily, I say unto you, the hour cometh, and now is, when the dead shall hear the voice of the Son of God; and they that hear shall live" (John 5. 24, 25).

But, fourthly, these signs are not all negative, recorded critically, pointing to the truth by correcting certain misunderstandings. Just as the healing of Bar-Timaeus in the synoptic Gospels seems to have been intended to show that Jesus bestows the true sight that will ultimately lead his disciples to apprehend the truth, so the healing of the man born blind anticipates the worship of the Church. This man, whose sight Jesus has restored, when told that he is confronted by the Son of God, says, "Lord, I believe" — and worships him (John 9. 38). He has, it has been said, "passed from Judaism to Christianity — and passes out of the story as the typical believer, the worshipper of God in Spirit and in truth". Here we see how those who witnessed them should have understood the healing acts of Jesus from the first, and what they should have been led by them to do.

Finally, the last of the signs of the fourth Gospel is the raising of Lazarus. It is a real restoration to life — about that there was no doubt in the evangelist's mind. It is, moreover, wrought out of compassion, in answer to a show of faith on the part of Mary and Martha, that has moved further towards Christian faith than the so-called faith of the crowds, though it has not yet attained to it. At the command of Jesus, Lazarus comes forth from the tomb — and also disappears from the story, for he has served his purpose. The process of death and corruption which is working in him, as in all creation, has for the time being been arrested and reversed. He is therefore a supreme parable of God's contrary, saving action bringing life out of death. But Lazarus disappears, because the real *locus* of the parable, the point where once and for all it is to be wrought out in actual fact — now with eternal consequences — is the point of the death and resurrection of Jesus. And for this reason, when Lazarus has been raised from the dead, the hostility of the Jews, already kindled by the healing of the man born blind, makes the story move rapidly and relentlessly towards Calvary. The hour is at hand — the point upon which all these outward signs are, by the eye of faith, seen to converge; the point that establishes them as significant and real. This is the hour of the death of Christ. It is also the hour of his glorification.

Healing in the New Testament

4

A double pattern runs through the Gospels, and through the whole New Testament. In relation to the acts of healing and exorcism, it can be described like this. There is a visible cycle and an invisible cycle. In the visible cycle, Jesus is confronted by real need, by real distress. Movement towards Jesus shows a real confidence in him, a confidence which he meets by a real satisfaction of the need. Not for one moment does the New Testament question the importance of this visible cycle. But the visible cycle ought to have caused men to apprehend the invisible cycle: the ultimate need of men who are dying, every one of them, in sin; the faith in God's imminent and universal action for their eternal salvation, which should be evoked by the presence of Jesus Christ; and God's ultimate satisfaction of all men's ultimate need in and through Jesus Christ—salvation, life from the dead, eternal union with God, glory. But *these two cycles must be held together closely, indeed inseparably*. Concentrate on the first alone—the visible cycle of experience; and real though it is, it holds out no hope, no ultimate reality, no true substance. To depress Jesus, or his Church, into this world only, to offer him as the mere source of health in time and space, is to misunderstand him altogether—altogether, and all the more tragically, because what he did in this world *should* be the means of understanding him. For, though there are many other ways as well, it is through the needs we really experience on earth, through our mental and physical distress, and through the compassionate ministry to men of one in the same situation as ourselves—through the spectacle of the satisfaction of distress which he undoubtedly bestowed—that our hearts and minds should be being drawn to faith, to the worship of Jesus as the Son of God, and to acceptance of the eternal life which he offers us. For those who have been given this faith, throughout the history of the Church as in the primitive Church of New Testament times, healings, like many other experiences in time and space, may light up with further meaning as manifestations of the glory of God in the face of Jesus Christ. But, ever since Jesus was rejected by his own people and misunderstood even by his own disciples, the royal road to understanding is through the spectacle of Christ lifted up upon the cross, *where there is no visible healing*, and this is presented to us primarily through the preaching and life of the Church (cf. Gal. 3. 1 etc.).

5

This rapid glance at the New Testament evidence makes it difficult to believe that our Lord regarded his healing miracles as illustrations of some general law, for instance, of the power of the human mind over the body: all that he did he conceived to be done only by the power of God. Nor does the New Testament suggest that this power is always available to men, as a sort of supernatural element in time and space. Throughout the New Testament, Jesus is represented as mediating the power of God at one supreme point in history, through his death and resurrection — although, through faith, his death and resurrection can exert this power at any point. Confidence in Jesus on the visible plane is important, since it points to the possibility of true faith, but the conception of "faith-healing", in a modern sense, is entirely foreign to the New Testament. And although, in the New Testament, sickness is a sign and a symptom of sin and is therefore related to sin, Jesus is said to have explicitly rejected the older view (already rejected in the book of Job) that all sickness is punishment for sin (Luke 13. 1-5; John 9. 1-3). Still less does there seem to be any ground in the New Testament for supposing that suffering is *intended* to be creative — an idea that seems to rest on a misunderstanding of the Passion of Jesus, which is represented rather as making room for the glory of God than as a human act of suffering that achieved glory for itself. Yet this does not mean that, when humbly accepted with faith in Christ, suffering, like any other human experience, may not be made spiritually creative by God's grace.

Granted the validity of the New Testament conception of acts of healing, Christians might try to bring home to themselves what it means in some such way as this. Because we live in the same world, and for many of us the first intimations of man's ultimate distress come through the spectacle or experience of physical or mental distress, Christians will try to see such distress as met by nothing less than the disclosure of its final implication and the assurance of the final glory with which God meets, and clothes, faith in Christ. Of this, if we had the eyes of Christ, the healing work of the medical profession would be a parable, even though its members necessarily work professionally with their eyes focused only on what men can measure and observe. Christians must try to focus their eyes, through time and space, on God. If unrelated to the final satisfaction of human need which is eternal life through Christ, laying on of hands, anointing with oil, even prayer for the sick, can have no meaning or purpose at all. In themselves, unrelated to God's final glory, such actions smack of magic. But if these outward signs, this privilege of intercession, are given by God in order that they may confront men with his eternal salvation in his Son, then use them Christians must, wherever they can, though always in the context of the Gospel of Christ crucified and risen, with the confession and absolution of sin—that is, with the recognition of man's ultimate need; with faith in the true sense of the word—that is, looking for God's ultimate salvation. Therefore they will never present these gifts of God as having any objective short of eternal life through Christ. They will never commend them as alternatives to medical action, or as supplementing the work of physicians or surgeons; least of all as in any sense *guaranteeing* observable results, on the cruel condition "Provided you have sufficient faith". Christians need not doubt that God will give results. They will pray that, whether God gives or withholds the permanent physical or mental restoration for which the physicians or surgeons are working; or whether he gives only a temporary restoration, permitting the patient to prepare himself more fully to maintain his faith in the hour of death; or whether he seems to give nothing at all— whatever the outcome it may become his means of grace. Christians have to try to see this world and God's ultimate world as Jesus did; and to fail to accept and to use the fundamental experiences of this world as means of the salvation of God and the gift of eternal life would be to separate and to secularize just where Jesus himself consecrated into one single oblation.

© F. N. Davey, 1964.

4

BELIEVING THE MIRACLES AND PREACHING THE RESURRECTION [1]

M. C. PERRY

I

How do we decide whether the Biblical miracles happened? The first thing to settle is the author's intention. When the Psalmist (114. 4) tells us that, at the Exodus, the mountains skipped like rams, we can easily distinguish between poetry and miracle. Similarly, we applaud Kepler for realizing that the point of the story of the sun's standing still (Josh. 10. 12f) lay, not in its bearing on the current Copernican-Ptolemaic dispute, but in the fact that the day was long enough for the Israelite victory; [2] and we realize that naturalists who legitimize the Book of Jonah by telling us which fish are capable of anthropophagy and regurgitation are wasting their learning on misapplied piety.

The historical value of the evidence is the next thing to look at. We know that Jonah was intended as a parable. Mark's story of the cursing of the fig-tree was not; but we can guess from a Lucan parable that the miracle has evolved from the story (Mark 11. 12-14, 20ff; Luke 13. 6-9).[3] We may also guess that there is a similar con-

[1] Reprinted from the *Expository Times*, lxxiii, August 1962, pp. 340-3, and lxiv, November 1963, p. 58-61, published by T. & T. Clark, Edinburgh.

[2] See John Dillenberger, *Protestant Thought and Natural Science*, 1961, p. 84.

[3] Though see J. N. Birdsall in the *Expository Times*, lxxiii, March 1962, p. 191, and A. de Q. Robin in *New Testament Studies*, viii, April 1962, pp. 276-81.

nection between Luke's parable of a man named Lazarus who dies and may not return to earth because "If they hear not Moses and the prophets, neither will they be persuaded, if one rise from the dead", and John's miracle of Lazarus who does rise from the dead and whose witness leads, not to persuasion, but to persecution, on the part of the authorities (Luke 16. 19-31; John 11. 1-44; 12. 10).[4] Perhaps in the puzzling story of the coin in the fish's mouth (Matt. 17. 24-7) we have caught a parable in the very act of becoming transformed into a miracle.

But when we have done these two things, what are we to make of the remainder, those miracles which are recorded as historical events and are as well attested historically as the non-miraculous happenings in whose matrix they are embedded? Thoroughgoing scepticism and thoroughgoing credulity are alike indefensible. The former relies on common sense, which is only shorthand for "the way of looking at things which comes naturally to a person conditioned by twentieth-century Western scientific materialism". We cannot let God be bound by what we think he ought to be allowed to do. He is not so small as to allow either scientists or theologians to dictate to him. But neither can we say, "If you believe in God, you will believe in his omnipotence. To believe in God and not the miracles is to strain at the gnat when you have already swallowed the camel." This puts all the Biblical miracles on the same footing and makes no distinction between an obviously secondary miracle like making iron swim and an obviously crucial one like the Resurrection. It completely bypasses the question of whether the miracles are well attested historically, and it cannot answer the question, "If these miracles, why not those of the Apocryphal Gospels or the legends of the saints?", except by appealing to a doctrine of literal inerrancy applied to an arbitrary Canon. Omnipotence means, not that God can do all things (he cannot deny himself—see 2 Tim. 2. 13) but that his purpose cannot be ultimately thwarted. "We should not conclude God doth things because he is able, but . . . should inquire what he hath done."[5]

What, then? Historical evidence alone cannot settle the question, because the type of event to which the evidence bears witness will

---

[4] See, however, R. Dunkerley in *New Testament Studies*, v. [1959], 321-7.

[5] Tertullian *adv. Prax.*, quoted by More & Cross, *Anglicanism*, 1935, p. 469.

itself determine whether that evidence is regarded as sufficient to warrant belief. Let me give an example. You have been spending the afternoon in the garden putting in wallflowers. With a feeling of satisfaction you look at the neat rows and freshly-raked soil, and go indoors for a wash and brush-up and a pair of slippers. As you sit by the fire with the paper, in comes your wife to say that the next-door dog has got in and is scratching around for bones. You are up again in a flash. The information is so intrinsically likely that you do not wait for confirmation. If, on the other hand, she tells you that the garden is full of unicorns, all nibbling the tops off the plants you have just put in, you murmur, "Yes dear; now pull the other one", and go back to the sports page. You know there are no such things as unicorns, and until you see one for yourself you stay in your chair. The amount of evidence is the same in each case, but your acceptance of it depends on your presuppositions. The more intrinsically unlikely the event, the more evidence you ask for. The best evidence is that of your own eyes. But even that is not sufficient for some events. When confronted with them, we immediately assume that there must be a catch somewhere. For instance, here (with my italics) is the opinion of the nineteenth-century physicist Helmholtz on telepathy:

> Neither the testimony of all the Fellows of the Royal Society, *nor even the evidence of my own senses*, could lead me to believe in the transmission of thoughts from one person to another independently of the recognized channels of sensation.[6]

That smacks of Hume's dictum, in his *Inquiry Concerning Human Understanding*, "that no human testimony can have such force as to prove a miracle". Nowadays we are prepared to believe in telepathy on sufficient evidence. Because no evidence was sufficient for Helmholtz, we call him prejudiced. Why damn him and not the disbeliever in unicorns? Because telepathy did not make sense on his *Weltanschauung* and could not be fitted into any system of thought, it was easier to deny it. And unless we have a system of thought that allows the Biblical miracles, we, too, shall find that to ignore the evidence is the only tolerable thing. It will be more likely that someone was mistaken than that our whole fabric of thought is wrong.

[6] Quoted by H. G. Baynes in *Journal of the Society for Psychical Research*, xlvi, 1941, p. 379.

and Preaching the Resurrection

The person who believes in Jesus' teaching and Crucifixion because the former makes moral sense and the latter, historical sense, but refuses to believe in the Resurrection because it does not make scientific sense, is using his reason to discriminate between items *all of which are equally well evidenced*. If we want to commend the historicity of the Resurrection (or of any other miracle) on the evidence available, we have to show how it can make sense, or give a world-picture into which it can fit. If we can do that, then our Biblical evidence has become respectable and may be accepted.

There are two ways of going about this. The first is to fit the miracles into the commonly received scientific world-picture and show how the received account could be explained without invoking otherwise unheard-of phenomena. For example, Flinders Petrie [7] showed how the plagues of Egypt could be explained as the natural order of events, beginning with the unwholesome stagnant Nile full of red organisms and dead fish in early June, and ending with the devastations of the plague which carried off the firstborn in the following April. Many people, on reading his account, may think that the explanation requires propitious coincidence to be miraculously accommodating. This it is. A miracle is not necessarily "something scientifically impossible". If it were, God could only reveal himself by the abnormal. He is not so clumsy a workman; and the Old Testament itself is a testimony to the fact that he is a God who can be known through history.

When we are fitting miracles into a scientific world-picture, we should not neglect the evidence of parapsychology. This may help to make credible alike the prescience of the prophets and the clairaudience of Elisha, who "telleth the king of Israel the words that thou speakest in thy bedchamber" (2 Kings 6. 12). But it is easily overdone.[8] Widengren has even used parapsychology to explain the way in which Ezekiel, like a psychic apport, was lifted up by his locks and transported bodily from Jerusalem to Tel-Abib, where (not unnaturally) he "sat there astonied among them seven

---

[7] *Egypt and Israel* [1911], 35 f., quoted by Gabriel Hebert, *When Israel came out of Egypt*, 1961, p. 69.

[8] Most people think that the late C. L. Tweedale and G. Maurice Elliot overdid it.

days" (Ezek. 3. 12-15; 8. 3).⁹ The incident puts as great a strain on our credulity as it must have done on the prophet's hair, and his flight is more likely to have been only one of poetic fancy; but there it is.

If we are not able to do this with a miracle (and only then) we must fall back on arguments of a purely theological nature, by trying to fit the miracle into a wider picture, to show that it is the sort of thing that we should expect God to do, and that it is of sufficient importance within the scheme of man's redemption for him to employ unusual methods to do it. Take, as example, the Virgin Birth. Here is a miracle (concede the point, please, if only for the sake of the argument) which is scientifically impossible. Can we none the less see it as theologically fitting? The Incarnation of God as Man was a new creation. It was as great and as new as that original Day when God said, "Let there be light", and there was light; when the morning stars sang together and all the sons of God shouted for joy. So it was only seemly that in this new creation, as in the old, the only part man should play was the passive one of receiving the miracle of grace. It is this sort of argument that will render the evidence for the Virgin Birth worthy of credibility; an argument about the possibility of human parthenogenesis only misses the point. We need to look deeper than the fact in order to find the meaning.

This type of approach, however, needs to be used as sparingly as possible. Not that we are all sceptics at heart, and prefer a scientifically explicable to a theologically explicable miracle, but for at least three reasons.

1. Gaps in a world of scientific explicability have a disconcerting habit of shrinking until the miracle is squeezed out of them; and with the gap goes the God who is the God of that gap.

2. God can be—and, indeed, most usually is—active within the very *normalness* of things. The more we multiply abnormal miracles, the easier it is to see God as a celestial tinker, and the less easy it is to see him in ordinary events.

3. This process of theological justification leaves tremendous scope for subjectivity of judgement. For instance, do we justify

⁹ G. Wildengren, *Literary and Psychological Aspects of the Hebrew Prophets*, 1948, p. 110; quoted by O. Eissfeldt in *The Old Testament and Modern Study*, ed. H. H. Rowley, 1951, p. 144.

the Virgin Birth along the lines I sketched above, or do we do so on an Augustinian view which treats marital intercourse as sinful and therefore unbefitting either our Lady or the conception of her Son? Do we see the Feeding of the Multitude as a pointer to Christ Jesus, the spiritual Bread who satisfies countless hungry souls (eucharistically or otherwise), or do we see it as teaching the lesson

> If we were all brothers, and loved one another
> The whole wide world could be fed
> On only two little fishes
> And five loaves of bread?

We said above that we had to decide on the intention of the writer when coming to a verdict on the historicity of the miracles he records. Behind his intention (to write history or poetry or parable) is his theology, and it may be that we shall reject the miracle when we find that it can have no orthodox theological justification. Behind the miracle of a person who is being crucified keeping silence, feeling no pain,[10] is a Docetic theology which does not square with our belief in the Word made flesh. It would be a miracle if iron were to float (2 Kings 6. 6—unless the narrative merely means that the prophet fished the axe-head out with the stick he cut down), but the intention here is plain; most of the Elisha stories are popular hagiographical attempts at going one better than Elijah. Theology is swallowed up in thaumaturgy. The same is true of stories like that of the child Jesus lengthening a piece of wood miscut by Joseph.[11] We reject these, not because we are sceptics, nor because they are not in the Bible, but because they do not fit in with the character of God. (Most of them are also shaky from the historical point of view; but that is not the point here.) The same would have been true of the miracle Jesus refused to work for the Pharisees. The world was full enough of wonder-workers. What it wanted was the coming of the Kingdom of God.

Conversely, if we have adequate theological reasons for *accepting* a miracle, this, too, will react back on our verdict about the value of the historical evidence. It will not turn secondary accretions into first-rate evidence, but, other things being equal, we shall

---

[10] *Gospel of Peter*, 4. 11 (M. R. James, *Apocryphal New Testament*, p. 91).

[11] *Gospel of Thomas*, 13 (M. R. James, *Apocryphal New Testament*, pp. 52-3).

favour the received account (for example) of the empty tomb on Easter morning rather than talk in terms of miracle-mongering additions to an original story. But this is only to repeat what we have already said about "fitting-in" as affecting the value rather than the amount of the evidence.

On the other hand, perfectly orthodox doctrine can help to create a miracle-story. What are we to say of the earthquake at the Crucifixion which opened some tombs so that three days later (but not before) their occupants were to be seen walking abroad? The very clumsiness of the story (Matt. 27. 51-3) shows it was intended as an illustration of the doctrine that Christ was the holder of the keys of death and hell (Rev. 1. 18) yet the firstborn from the dead (Col. 1. 18; Rev. 1. 5), so that the person responsible for initiating the story assumed that "this sort of thing must have happened".

What, now, about miracles where part of the underlying doctrine is "a prophecy has been fulfilled"? How about the healing of the man who was μογιλάλος in Mark 7. 32 (fulfilling Isa. 35. 6) or, in some people's view, the Virgin Birth itself, based upon the LXX of Isa. 7. 14? This depends (a) on whether we believe that the existence of a prophecy is sufficient cause for God to see to its fulfilment (and, if so, what are we to say about the unfulfilled prophecies? Go after the latest Joanna Southcott?) and (b) on the historical question of whether anyone would have invented a miracle in order to prove such a fulfilment. Both views have been held. It is more likely that there were many healings of stammerers and that this one has been deliberately referred to its Isaianic foreshadowing by the evangelist for his doctrinal purposes.

I may have implied earlier that it could be possible to give either a purely scientific or a purely theological account of a miracle. The last few paragraphs should have shown the dangers of an attempt at being so rigid in our distinctions. A "factual" account alone can never be satisfactory, as there is no revelation in an account without a meaning. We cannot separate historicity and significance. We must ask our "Why?" Why did God let *this* striking coincidence happen? Why did God suspend the normal workings of Nature on *that* occasion? If we are blinded by the unusual nature of the event, we shall see τέρατα rather than σημεῖα —wonders rather than signs. We should ask people, not whether they can swallow certain events, but whether they can justify them. Similarly for the unhistorical miracles. When we have dismissed an incident as legendary, we have not finished with it. Why did the writer (who, we presume, had *something* to teach us about God) invent or perpetuate this story?

If we turn our attention from history to meaning, we may be able to discover something *about* God instead of continually trying to prove that he *could* do what he *has* done. Too much apologetic is on the defensive and therefore starts with a psychological handicap. Start from the premise that God exists and acts; begin to draw up a theology on that basis; and it will be found to be a more convincing method than starting with a world in which God has no place and arguing him into it. It may then be that the Living God will be able to break the bounds of the written word and the past tense, and to become incarnate in us and our hearers.

To sum up our argument so far. Faced with an account of a miracle, we should first

(*a*) find out whether the writer intended us to take it literally, and then

(*b*) see whether it is as well-evidenced historically as the non-miraculous matrix which we accept as factual.

If the story survives these tests, there are two types of consideration which will affect whether we take it as true.

(*a*) Is it credible on a scientific world-view?

(*b*) Is it in accord with the totality of Christian theology?

On its own, (*a*) isolates the fact from the meaning (and *may* imply belief in an impotent God), whereas (*b*) alone needs, for a variety of reasons, to be used with caution and as a last resort. Most miracles need both approaches, but so much of our apologetic has been concerned with (*a*) that we have tended to forget the way in which (*b*) affects belief in a miracle. We should not be afraid of jettisoning (*a*) if driven to it.

But this formula is no "Open sesame" to the problem of believing in and commending the miracles. We cannot strait-jacket ourselves by producing a single inflexible approach to every miracle-story. Each of us will have to wrestle his own way through to his own solution, and each miracle needs to be considered separately. It will be the purpose of the second half of this essay to look at the Resurrection in the light of what has been written above.

II

"I BELIEVE, what I have proved, his Resurrection to be a Piece of Fraud, and his other Miracles to have been all Artifice." Thomas Woolston's *Discourses on the Miracles* were forthright and certain enough; yet a contemporary Bishop [12] had no difficulty in coming to the opposite conclusion. How, when they both depended on the same Gospel sources?

It is the same in the 1960s as the 1720s. Christian writers who defend the integrity of the Gospel narratives of the Resurrection seem to have little success except among those who start out wanting to believe.

How do we convince the modern sceptic that the Resurrection happened? The historical method [13] is to show that the narratives hang together in a convincing way and that all possible alternative explanations run into hidden snags. "When", to quote Sherlock Holmes, "you have eliminated the impossible, whatever remains, *however improbable*, must be the truth." This method rarely convinces, because what remains in the case of the Resurrection is not an improbability but an impossibility. To the sceptic, there are no such things as resurrections; it is easier to postulate an unconcealed error vitiating the whole records.

The "scientific method" goes a step further by quoting parallels to show that the Gospel events are not impossibilities.[14] But since the case-books of psychical research are themselves as puzzling as the Biblical records, and "telepathic hallucination" is little more than a term used to cloak our ignorance, we are not greatly helped. Parapsychological data may help convince the man who says, "I cannot believe the Evangelists because nothing like the stories they relate has ever happened in the world at any other time", but as *explanations* of the Resurrection, they are merely an example of *obscurum per obscurius*. They would not convert a modern Woolston. All they could do would be to convince a man of the external facts. Faith in the Resurrection is more than believing that

---

[12] Thomas Sherlock (1678-1761), Bishop successively of Bangor, Salisbury and London, and author in 1729 of the *Tryal of the Witnesses of the Resurrection of Jesus*.

[13] E.g., in Frank Morison's *Who Moved the Stone?*

[14] See, e.g., G. Zorab, *Het Opstandingsverhaal in het Licht der Parapsychologie* (The Hague, 1949) and M. C. Perry, *The Easter Enigma* (London, 1959).

the disciples were not deluded, and even if we could bring a man to concede that the external events were not unlikely to have happened as recorded, we could not force him to go further and say, "I believe what it *means*". This is where our wider or theological world-view comes in. The facts do not imply the meaning, but without some kind of meaning the facts are not worth the bother of believing. The meaning to be drawn out of the facts need not be a Christian one, but the Christian will claim that the meaning in which he believes makes the best sense of the facts and gives a unity to his whole theology. Let us look at various ways in which the Resurrection appearances might be fitted in as a necessary part of a larger picture so that they can become significant enough to be worth believing.

1. According to some people, the appearances prove that a human being can survive death. On this view, it does not matter *who* appeared; the Resurrection simply takes its place among the data of psychical research, and it is a very humble place, because there are many other cases of much higher evidential value. It is, indeed, doubtful whether the narratives prove even as much as is claimed, because many people would be content to explain even the best-evidenced of present-day anecdotal material in psychical research without recourse to the unlikely hypothesis of survival.

2. This first view is simply anthropological. If we are able to preach the Resurrection as a part of Christian doctrine, God must have a place in it. Can we say that Jesus was the supremely good man who remained faithful to death and was rewarded by God with the gift of immortality? 'If so, then only the "unco' guid" have any hope of being raised, and we are of all men most miserable.

3. That was theology, but not *Christian* theology. The key to our problem is in our doctrine of the Person of Christ. To say "Jesus is God" would make the Resurrection quite understandable. God cannot die—of course the Resurrection happened. But it can have nothing to say about the destiny of men, because God is God and man is man. The Resurrection may show Jesus as the living contemporary of every dying generation, but although Jesus lives, we shall not.

4. But then, "Jesus is God" ignores the Incarnation, and any view short of full Christian orthodoxy makes the Resurrection unpreach-

able and unbelievable. We cannot rest content until we find a view which involves the Resurrection in all the major Christian doctrines and binds them into a unity. Anything which leaves the Resurrection as a disconnected doctrine will be ultimately unsatisfying.

A popular approach, especially among the devotees of "Biblical Theology", is that *via* the themes of the Two Ages. The Resurrection was supremely unexpected. Pilate and Caiaphas could settle down to a calm night's sleep and the disciples would (like Martha, John 11. 24) only expect him to "rise again in the resurrection at the last day". Resurrection is a thing of the Last Day, not a thing to be expected (even of the Christ) in the here and now. They had not grasped that when ἤγγικεν ἡ βασιλεία τοῦ Θεοῦ, the Last Age had dawned and they were now living in "the overlap of the ages" (cf. 1 Cor. 10. 11). This tells us that the Resurrection is an act of God, but the concept of the Two Ages does little to explain or illuminate it. More important, it has no *necessary* connection with the rest of our Incarnational and Trinitarian theology. It speaks of the acts of God *through* Christ but not necessarily of the act of God *in* Christ.

5. We may attempt to link Cross and Resurrection by claiming that without the Resurrection, the Cross would be a past act but, because of it, Christ "ever liveth" and is able to be the contemporary and Saviour of every man. The Resurrection makes it possible to apply subjectively to each individual what the Cross has supplied objectively for all men.[15] But this robs the Cross of its finality and is not explicit enough in linking Incarnation with Resurrection. Admittedly Incarnation is involved in soteriology, but one could wish for a clearer link between Christology and the Easter faith.

6. We must therefore interpret the Resurrection in terms of the full Christian faith concerning the nature of Christ; and we shall be relieved to find that St Paul has already done it for us.

According to Paul, Adam was created good but because of his transgression his offspring have been hereditarily befouled. All men are in Adam, in whom all die (1 Cor. 15. 22; cf. Rom. 5. 12). To be released from this bondage, we must return to God. Our state of

---

[15] F. Prat, *La Théologie de S. Paul*[7], Paris 1923, Vol. ii. pp. 250-6, as quoted by D. M. Stanley, *Christ's Resurrection in Pauline Soteriology*, Rome 1961, pp. 10-11.

being "in Adam" means we cannot do this of ourselves; we must first come into union with someone whose Godward act is at least as powerful and fecund as Adam's sinward one. This "someone" is Christ (Rom. 5. 17f). Adam was the first of the old humanity as Christ is of the new. If we are "in Christ" who has risen, we share thereby his immortality—but not for our own merits, any more than we were in the old covenant of death for our individual sins. It is all a matter of solidarity.

How can Jesus be this super-Adamic figure? Here is the crucial importance of the Incarnation within the doctrine of the Resurrection. As man, Jesus was born in Adam, yet by rendering to God that perfect obedience even unto death which God desires (but has never had) from the sons of Adam, he has broken Adam's covenant of bondage. This righteous act is effective to others because Jesus is not only man but representative man, so that his actions affect the whole of human nature. They do more; because *God* was in Christ, his act of righteousness not only restores man's true humanity for all those who are "in him", it also opens up the possibility of their divinization. God became man as never to be unmade more, in order to lift humanity to God as never again to sink (cf. 1 John 3. 2 with 2 Cor. 3. 18). All humanity is potentially affected by this act, but nobody is affected automatically. The new life in Christ has to be consciously and deliberately entered into by each individual, by baptism, whereas (see Rom. 5) a man belongs involuntarily in Adam by reason of his birth. By baptism a man dies to Adam and is reborn in Christ (Rom. 6. 2-5), and he is maintained within this solidarity by living in the Church his body (Eph. 1. 22, 23) and partaking of his body the Eucharist (1 Cor. 10. 16ff). So our destiny is linked to Christ's experiences. "One died for all, therefore all died" (2 Cor. 5. 14). We "put off the old man . . . and put on the new" (Col. 3. 9f) by the death and resurrection of baptism (Rom. 6. 5). The new life is ours now but will be consummated in a resurrection body in the life of the world to come (1 Cor. 15).

This way of looking at things has the advantage of basing our doctrine of the Resurrection firmly on our Christology; but the Pauline terms we have been using will cut little ice to-day. To-day's philosophical climate would regard as meaningless the concept of incorporation in terms of an abstract yet almost hypostasized "human nature" which Christ took upon him to transform for all after him who took that same human nature. We need to translate the doctrine before we can preach the Resurrection to-day.

We do not mind thinking of a mythological figure like Adam as representative. To talk about "solidarity in Adam" is only a highfalutin theological way of saying "human beings behave like this". But Jesus Christ is not mythological; he is historical. Paul was not worried; so (for him) was Adam. If Adam's historical existence did not stop him being mythologically representative, no more should Christ's. The historical Adam was the first man, whose hereditary influence passed to all his descendants. Christ is the first of the "new men" and his influence passes similarly, except that Adam's heredity is a physical matter while Christ's is spiritual. We, of course, will have none of this. Not only are acquired characteristics uninheritable; not only does it only work if there was an historical Adam; not only is the parallel between Adam and Christ shaky in the extreme; but the whole notion of "spiritual heredity" is unobservable, indefinable, and therefore meaningless.

The only way out is to recognize that Paul has clothed the existential facts of human and Christian experience in the language of myth. "Incorporation into Christ's new life through baptism" is a mythological way of saying what Christ—an historical figure—has done for Paul; and "solidarity in death for every man born into this world" similarly expresses what Adam—*believed to be* an historical figure—implies for him.

The Pauline formulation (however we re-express it in modern terms) shows the place of the Resurrection in a single theological synthesis in which creation, incarnation, and redemption all have their place. By it we "attain unto the *unity* of the faith, and of the knowledge of the Son of God, unto a fullgrown man, unto the measure of the stature of the fullness of Christ" (Eph. 4. 13). This unification of the miracle of the Resurrection within the totality of a theology of which it forms a necessary part is what is meant by showing that the Resurrection "fits into a wider picture" and that therefore the miracle may be preached and defended without offending our theological sensibilities.

If, therefore, the Incarnation makes possible the solidarity of Christ and Christian by baptism, how do we preach this solidarity as we set forth the gospel of the Resurrection?

1. *Jesus died.* Enoch and Elijah were translated without seeing

death, but for Jesus, death was real. We may not minimize the significance of death by using pious soothing phrases. It is our last enemy (1 Cor. 15. 26) and though Christ has drawn its sting and deprived it of victory (1 Cor. 15. 55) we, like him, must die before we can rise (Eph. 4. 9). There is the symbolic death of baptism (Rom. 6. 4) and the metaphorical "putting to death" of our earthly passions (Col. 3. 5), but there is also the real and agonizing experience of what Teilhard has called "the passivity of diminishment" coming to its climax in the passivity of our death. We must not expect to be spared this, but Christ is with us and he can turn it for us into the gate of new life.

2. *Jesus rose.* Jairus' daughter, the widow's son, and Lazarus were brought back from death and returned into this same life of change and decay in which they would eventually grow old and die again. Jesus *rose*—to an endless life, unmarked by the imperfections and unsatisfactoriness of this present age. We, with him, are raised into a new quality of life. If heaven were only earth prolonged, everlasting life might be more bad news than good, and would deserve that most withering of teenagers' scornful remarks—"how *boring*".

3. *Jesus was raised.* In the New Testament [16] it is always ὁ Θεὸς ἤγειρεν, ἠγέρθη Χριστός. It is not as though Jesus had immortality as a basic human possession (this is only true of God— see 1 Tim. 6. 16). Here is a mighty act of the living God, in the power of the Resurrection (Phil. 3. 10). There is no natural immortality for men, but if we are raised, "we shall live with him through the power of God" (2 Cor. 13. 4; cf. 1 Cor. 6. 14). There will be no more ineffectuality in our living, because the power by which we live is God's, not ours.

4. *Jesus is risen.* We cannot speak of the Resurrection, or preach it, in the past tense. Jesus Christ is risen—to-day! He meets us just as really as he met his disciples in the Upper Room or on the Emmaus Road. He may not always be recognized—if our eyes are not opened, we may only see a stranger on the road, someone needing our help and our companionship. But in them, Christ confronts us with the claim of a living person. The doctrine of the Resurrection is not weak and sentimental comfort, useful only for

---

[16] The exception is 1 Thess. 4. 14; and compare John 10. 17f.

mourners at the graveside. It involves a call to service as real as that of the Risen Christ in the Gospels (*vide* Matt. 28. 19 or John 20. 21). And as Jesus is alive, so can we be. "He that hath the Son hath the life" (1 John 5. 12; cf. John 3. 15f). The tense is present; there is no need to wait.

5. Finally, *Jesus has a body*. The doctrine of the immortal soul which slips from its outworn physical husk at death is not Christian. The body is for the Lord (1 Cor. 6. 13). Not necessarily the flesh and blood body (1 Cor. 15. 50), but some form of expression there must be, with some form of continuity with what has gone before. Admittedly here the parallel between Jesus and ourself breaks down. His flesh and blood body disappeared from the earth. Ours will not, but we may follow Paul in believing that we have a "spiritual body" which will be revealed when our present flesh and bood covering has been removed from it (2 Cor. 5. 1ff). No Christian should neglect, or suppress, or pamper his body. If we are risen with Christ (Col. 3. 1-7) we are to treat our bodies in a Christian way, because if the seed is damaged, the flower may fail to open (1 Cor. 15). The Risen Life is life in a body, just as Christ lives in his body the Eucharist, and his body the Church. Our duty as we share in the risen life is to act in Christ's world and bring to bear on it the life of Jesus and the power of his resurrection.

Here is a gospel we can preach, because the Resurrection has been integrated into the whole of Christian theology and in a way which affects the living of the whole of the Christian life; and here is a gospel we can believe, because the Resurrection is seen to take its necessary place in the widest picture we can draw of matters human and divine. This therefore is a miracle we must commend to the whole world, urging its credibility by every means at our disposal.

© M. C. Perry, 1962, 1963.

5

INTIMATIONS OF IMMORTALITY IN THE THOUGHT OF JESUS [1]

HENRY J. CADBURY

THE historic Ingersoll lectureship on the Immortality of Man requires of the lecturer both some legitimate extension of its terms and some necessary limitation of his field. One is justified in supposing that the pious layman who planned the foundation was not thinking in highly technical terms, but like laymen of our day was thinking of a widely shared belief in the *post mortem* survival or revival of those who die. If he had wished to specify the indiscriminate persistence of the individual as a philosophical tenet of the nature of man, he could well have used the more familiar term—the immortality of the soul. On the other hand, if he had wished to be faithful to the wording of much of the Bible and to the Church's creeds, he would have spoken of the Resurrection of the Dead.

Earlier lecturers have taken the liberty of dealing with the nearest analogue to one or other of these concepts in a great variety of cultural situations. It has seemed to me not more out of bounds to inquire into what little evidence we have of the thought of Jesus in this area. The word immortality was perhaps not even known to him. It is scarcely an Aramaic concept. Even the whole Greek New Testament has the classical term but two or three times. What Jesus did apparently think of man's future, where his views

[1] The Ingersoll Lecture for 1959, reprinted from the *Harvard Theological Review*, Vol. LIII, No. 1, January 1960.

are likely to have come from, and particularly in what kind of context they seemed to him significant, are questions that are worthy of the brief mention that the present occasion permits.

Without overshadowing this limited subject I find it necessary or at least desirable to deal in advance and at some length with some modern and even some early Christian perspectives that are unlikely to have been shared by Jesus himself in order that we may be in a position to conjecture and to contrast his own way of thinking. To do so one must speak in somewhat general terms of the New Testament as a whole, a much less homogeneous body of thought, and of some problems of its interpretation. The disproportion of such prefatory matters may be remedied by the brevity with which the central subject can be presented.

A year ago in the Cambridge subway I was struck by an advertisement: "You don't need eyes to see God." I soon concluded it was not merely another text of religious propaganda, but a solicitation for medical purposes. I recalled that a friend of mine who had died lately in a Boston hospital had donated her eyes for transplanting to the living blind, and closer inspection of the small print of the notice confirmed my conjecture with the words, "Write or telephone to the Boston Eye Bank."

What interested me was the religious implication of the notice. It had been used, I learned, with the consent of the local Churches, including especially the Roman Catholic. It was also used presumably with the assumption that it would have meaning to the travelling public, beyond mere Church affiliation. Since the latest Gallup Poll to which I have access reported that 96% of the people of America believe in God and 76% believe in a life after death, the general acceptability of the slogan could be taken for granted.

Yet I can hardly believe it represents a clear or uniform view on the part of those who accept the slogan or who increasingly answer Dr Gallup's questions in the affirmative. The Biblical teaching is not clear whether either here or hereafter anyone sees God with these eyes. They are rather a figure of speech for what American theologians were calling a few years ago *New Eyes for Invisibles* or *Eyes of Faith*.[2] It should be easy for us therefore to

---

[2] Titles of books by Rufus M. Jones, 1943, and Paul S. Minear, 1946, respectively.

imagine a similar undefinedness in the first century Church among those who at that time took for granted both the belief in God and the belief in life after death.

The New Testament root of the latter was primarily the Jewish resurrection belief. This was based on the eschatological view of history such as is found in the books we call apocalypses. It is doubtful whether it occurs in the older books like Job and the Psalms,[3] though passages from both have been taken in the later sense, much as in the New Testament certain passages which do imply resurrection have had read into them the quite different doctrine of immortality. One Old Testament book, Koheleth, or Ecclesiastes, seems definitely to deny after life—in spite of the glorious, though perhaps mistranslated, text, "He hath set eternity in their heart" (3. 11).

If historical and critical studies are to be trusted, it was first in the Maccabean period that a special situation gave rise to a resurrection belief. There was a new hope of a better day near at hand. It was precipitated by persecution as hope often is, but the persecution raised a special problem. The martyrs who had been most loyal of all were likely to miss the consummation while the lukewarm of the lucky survivors might share it. The book of Daniel by a leap of faith, trusting in God's justice, declares: "Many of those that sleep in the dust of the earth shall awake, some to everlasting life, and some to shame and everlasting contempt" (12. 2).

There is a curious parallel in what is perhaps our oldest extant Christian document, 1 Thessalonians. Again the hope of a near *dénouement* burned with special brightness. Its imminence was calculated (as in Daniel), perhaps overcalculated. In the expectant group at Thessalonica some already had died. In addition to other reasons for sorrow their surviving friends saw no justice in their being cheated of the common Christian reward. So Paul consoles them with assurance:

> But we would not have you ignorant, brethren, concerning those who are asleep, that you may not grieve as others do who have no hope. For since we believe that Jesus died and rose again, even so, through Jesus, God will bring with him those who have fallen asleep. For this we declare to you by the word of the Lord, that we who are alive, who are left until the coming of the Lord, shall not precede

[3] Cf. most recently C. S. Lewis, *Reflections on the Psalms*, 1958, chapter 5.

those who have fallen asleep. For the Lord himself will descend from heaven with a cry of command, with the archangel's call, and with the sound of the trumpet of God. And the dead in Christ will rise first; then we who are alive, who are left, shall be caught up together with them in the clouds to meet the Lord in the air; and so we shall always be with the Lord. Therefore comfort one another with these words (1 Thess. 4. 13-18, R.S.V.).

As Paul says elsewhere (1 Cor. 15. 18), without such a promise one must conclude that those who have fallen asleep in Christ, i.e. deceased Christians, have perished.

Thus in both Old Testament and New Testament the resurrection belief enters as an exception, as a problem of a minority. But with the apocalyptic hope deferred the minority who have died or will die becomes a majority. What was exceptional was universalized, at least by one influential sect, the Pharisees, and by Christians, including perhaps in time Paul himself.

Another factor in the New Testament is the belief in the resurrection of Jesus. The relation of this to the wider belief is ambiguous. In fact the term resurrection is to-day often used confusedly, meaning now the individual instance of Jesus, now the anticipation of a wider occurrence. One is a past event, one is future. The past event is treated as a foretaste, or first fruits, of the future. Paul uses it as assurance of the future—briefly in 1 Thessalonians, more at length in 1 Corinthians. Whether he regarded it as occurring in the same form as the future one—and it is this which he principally is discussing in 1 Cor. 15—one cannot tell. If he did, the accounts in the gospels hardly agree with him. In fact, their view of the same body, scars and all, flesh and bones (Luke 24. 39; John 20. 25, 27; contrast "flesh and blood cannot inherit," etc., 1 Cor. 15. 50) is antithetical to what Paul says of the more general resurrection. The Corinthians who cavilled at Paul's teaching as incredible would find little satisfaction in the resurrection stories in the Gospels if they met them currently in circulation or read them later.

The experiences that led early Christians to believe Jesus was risen are obscure. They may have been partly related to the future expectation current in apocalyptic circles. If he was soon to take part as they expected in a final rôle it was natural to think he would rise ultimately, or indeed had risen and was in the interim *Messias absconditus*. More decisive for such a belief would be any kind of vivid sense that Jesus was still or again in contact with them — visible in heaven (Stephen in Acts), or on earth, or audible in dreams or visions (Paul in Acts). Even these are only causes for inferences to be made that he had risen. Whether the stories of the empty grave are inferences from these or whether the beliefs in his resurrection are inferences from the empty grave is uncertain. All these beliefs could arise in any order and would tend in the end to confirm one another.

Behind any or all of these is doubtless the current Jewish belief in resurrection of some people — not any belief in immortality, nor indeed a general resurrection nor what we should call to-day parapsychology or spiritualism. Whatever experience or convictions the first Christians had in connection with the Jesus who had been crucified would be conditioned by the current abstract resurrection belief if it were at all possible, and would be interpreted in its terms.

Conversely this single episode when so interpreted would immensely strengthen that same resurrection belief. It seemed to Paul in 1 Cor. 15 and elsewhere, and to his biographer in Acts, the strongest assurance. For others than Jesus resurrection was in the future, hence uncertain. With Jesus it was in the past, and "only the past is secure". But, along with the Holy Spirit, it was a guarantee of the future. Both of them are called "first fruits". The resurrection of Jesus sets the pattern for other cases. "As in Adam all die, so in Christ shall all be made alive." What Jesus and Paul and their contemporaries had come to accept in the abstract, now after Easter because of this single concrete instance, became more credible and more assured. Unlike the Jews, the Christians now could argue with more assurance for the extension of one certified phenomenon. What God had done God could do. This was a method of argument that non-Christian Jews and pagans could not withstand. Their only defence was to doubt or deny the resurrection of Jesus. Probably on this rather than on the general belief the controversy turned.

If what has been said in the preceding paragraphs is correct, we get something very much like arguing in a circle. If the *post mortem* experience of Jesus was interpreted in terms of the Jewish belief in the resurrection of the just, then the Christian belief in the latter rested in turn at least in part upon the former as so interpreted. Such a circular process ought not to disturb us or surprise us. Our trouble is that when we look at a group of long established beliefs we tend to forget their genetic character. Though we cannot always at this late date determine the sequence of their origin we should be prepared to believe that they once were either inferences from or presuppositions of one another. Their logical consistency is due precisely to this human process rather than to a more objective foundation. In such circumstances it becomes quite easy to argue in a circle, if that is the right way to describe the matter.

The effect of the belief in Jesus' resurrection on the early Christian belief in the wider resurrection experience can hardly be overestimated. It was the kind of assurance, contemporary and concrete, that the most ardent though speculative convictions of Pharisees or other non-Christian Jews could not have equalled. And it has played a major rôle in the continuing Christian hope.

But before leaving this factor in the subject one should remember how complicated were the forces at work in connection with the early Easter story. Even without the uncongenial or irreconcilable spiritualizing presentation by Paul, the gospel narratives themselves suggest contradiction or combination of more than one point of view or motive. The apologetic element is obvious, though like much apologetic of all kinds it tends to be inconsistent or even contradictory. The details given look sometimes like afterthoughts more than like the original sources of the convictions. This does nothing to reduce our certainty that Jesus' resurrection was firmly believed in, nor does it necessarily affect our historical judgement about what actually did or did not happen. There was no clear pattern in the underlying Jewish anticipation that would force the Christian story of Jesus' resurrection into a ready-made mould.

There were in fact other aspects of Judaism which both before and after the events of Easter the first Christians shared. 1. One of these was quite different from any resurrection belief—the belief that in individual instances men had escaped death altogether. They were quite literally immortal—not in the sense that having died once they would live forever, but in the sense that they had not died and perhaps would not die. Instead of death and descent into Sheol they had experienced removal—ascension, assumption,

in the Thought of Jesus

rapture, are the names theology has used—and the instances first noted by the Jews and Christians, though differently described, are Enoch, Elijah, and probably Moses. Elements of such belief are closely associated with Christian views of the resurrection, whether that of Jesus or that of Christians in general. In both of these real death was taken for granted. Indeed orthodox Christianity was concerned to stress—perhaps against docetism—that Jesus really died (Ignatius), and was buried (Paul, the Creeds), instead of being removed at once from the cross (Gospel of Peter) or before the cross to God and heaven. Instead of such prompt assumption, opportunity for appearances of the risen Jesus was required in a period of sojourn on earth whether forty days (Acts) or some briefer or much longer period. The ascension belief was not fully rejected. It was added to resurrection belief. It is implied not only in the explicit narrative in Acts 1, but in other passages of Luke-Acts, in John and Paul. There is no clear distinction between appearances of the risen Jesus that assume he has already been thus exalted and those which at least by context defer such exaltation.

2. Another aspect of pre-Christian belief which fits very neatly here and which also had, I believe, much to do with the Christian belief in the resurrection of Jesus is the expectation of the coming of the Messiah. In the nature of the case this expectation had no fixed features in Judaism, and various forms of it are reflected in the Gospels. Certainly some people held that when he came it would be after prior existence and not completely *de novo*, and others that the place from which he came was not a matter of general knowledge. Now early after Jesus' death and perhaps before, he was identified with this coming Messiah, and it was therefore natural that his availability for this future rôle should be indicated. Of course availability did not require an immediate resurrection. Fourth Ezra, a Jewish writing probably of the first Christian century, speaks of the Messiah as remaining dead for a long period. But the Christian Church, while it looked for the *parousia* in the quite imminent future, found in the view that the Messiah had been promptly raised (Does "the third day" of 1 Cor. 15. 4 and elsewhere not emphasize this promptness?) an assurance of this eschatological hope. Jesus was immediately available in the sense that he was not in Sheol or in the grave, but was in heaven or at God's right hand, whence in any case the events of the last

day were likely to be initiated. Thus the eschatological hope of Judaism was a conditioning factor not only for the pre-Christian and Christian belief in the plural resurrection "at the last day" but also for the particular Christian belief in the individual and exceptional prior resurrection of Jesus.

Perhaps the dependence of these Christian beliefs on the primitive Jewish-Christian eschatology is not generally realized by modern believers. This is, however, a minor embarrassment compared with the fact that the very notion of Messiahship is dependent on the same circle of ideas, and with it the core for any superlative view of the person and work of Jesus Christ. In so far as the primitive eschatology is outgrown or abandoned as myth, we must admit that modern beliefs in the significance of Jesus of Nazareth and also beliefs in his or our after life are by-products or survivals or developments of the archaic and outmoded dreams of the apocalyptic dreamers. There is nothing unusual in the persistence of partial elements of myth when the myth as a whole is discredited. If they persist by sheer inertia that is natural. But the thoughtful or conscientious Christian to-day will welcome the discovery of this ancestry in order that he may inquire further into the motives of their origin and the relevance of those motives for to-day.

Before we attempt to do so, something should be said about the word myth. It is somewhat ambiguous and is perhaps unnecessarily offensive. It is used of stories of the past, connected with religion, and aiming to explain the origin of beliefs or practices. This is not the sense in which I have employed it. It is also used of the future, of dreams or prophecies of what from the time of the mythmaker is yet to take place. In the nature of things the imaginative factor is in such predictions peculiarly strong. Actually they rarely use much of the available data for conjecturing what will probably happen. They are even more fallible than political forecasts based on public opinion polls or weather predictions made by scientific meteorologists. If they have validity it must be credited to the supernatural foresight of inspired prophets and seers. Natural calculation or astute insight would rarely be an acceptable explanation to religious believers in these myths.

There is a third sense in which to-day theologians seem to use the word or the root, though not of the narrative content of an idea so much as of its framework. It means the *Weltanschauung* in which people express themselves, whether about things past, things contemporary, or things future. Demythicizing (demythologizing) is the attempt to strip away from religious thought such elements as belong to transient and unscientific cosmology or psychology. In the former belongs the three-storey universe, the earth with heaven above and hell beneath, in the second belong the mythical beings like demons and angels.

If this process is justified as applied to narratives in the Gospels of the New Testament which appear to have a kernel of history, we can hardly object if it is applied to the purely futuristic ideas of life after death. That the dead become angels and exist in heaven would be the kind of mythical view that would be the first to disappear at the hands of modern demythologizing. Probably we are quite prepared to surrender heaven as a place literally in the sky, and the angels as corporeal beings with or without wings. The purpose of demythologizing is to remove the shell of such notions in order that the spiritual values can be preserved and translated into terms congenial to our own *Weltanschauung*, and existential, that is, relevant to our need.

One cannot, however, resist the temptation to ask why we stop the process of removal just where these scholars do. If some of the furnishings of religious setting in the past happen to be more congenial to the present, are they thereby the more real? Are not myth and symbol almost universal in religion, almost inevitable? The presence of the naïve and archaic in parts of the New Testament language ought rather to warn us of the same element of myth in the rest, even though we find it easier to accept.

"Poetry," writes a modern literary critic, "is the imaginative dominion over experience." The same can be said for religion. Religion tends to personalize and materialize its contents. It operates through dramatization. Beside angels and demons it has other characters, *dramatis personae*, God, Jesus, Satan, with whom men have to do. Their relationship to us is conceived much as of actors on a stage. The myth of *Heilsgeschichte* is an imaginative narration of describable transactions. It can be as definite as the plot of a novel, and fiction in turn can be as objective and realistic as the prose facts of history.

There are children who are particularly addicted to fantasy. With or without the use of dolls they live at times in a make-believe world of fictitious characters living in human fashion, with all the characteristic features of events in experience. Perhaps this persistence of imagination is one of the charming features of childhood that Wordsworth had in mind in his famous ode. And imagination naturally plays its part in thinking of life after death. But we must recognize precisely that it is imagination and that its figures are taken—whether mystical or existentialist—from other scenes. As it was in the days of Noah, so shall it be in the days of the Son of Man, and so it is in childhood's fantasy: they eat, they drink, they buy and sell, they marry or are given in marriage. I am not concerned now to challenge the legitimacy and value of all such symbolic aspects of religion. It is only fair to ask that they be recognized, and recognized within the cautious line of what is called reality as well as beyond it.

It has already been mentioned that demythologizing is somewhat destructive of certain categories of space, the ancient Semitic view of a universe in layers. But another ancient category and one not obsolete is the category of time. Our Jewish-Christian tradition is especially given to this. One need merely be reminded of the use of age, or ages. Time extends from the age to the ages of the ages. Life for men is in this age and then in the age to come. History may be described in the book of reigns (as the Greek entitles our Book of Kings). The supreme ideal is described in a time word—the reign of God. It is perhaps characteristic of the difference between the Hellenic and Semitic, that when they symbolize value concretely the former tends to do so geographically, the latter chronologically.

In Christianity both ancient and modern the category of time has played a large part. Religion is understood as revealed in history. God deals with men in successive dispensations, and is known by his actions in time. The past set of covenants which form the framework of the Pentateuch share this outlook as does the simpler division of history that one finds in Paul. In the first the events are the Sabbath (Creation), kosher food (Noah), circumcision (Abraham), the final law (Moses). For Paul the intervals are "from Adam to Moses", from Moses to Christ, and until Christ's return.

In modern Christianity the same temporal representations are favoured. The concept of evolution has made them attractive to liberal and secular thinkers. There is little criticism of the linear concept of the Old Testament or New as applied to time to match the demythologizing of the spatial concepts of vertically separated levels. In general, "Biblical theology" seems to have given the time element a new lease of life. Cullmann's title, *Christ and Time*,[4] is topical, and so are the overtones of phrases like *Heilsgeschichte* and "Christ event." Von Hügel described the Fourth Gospel quite differently. He says of it, "There is everywhere a striving to contemplate history *sub specie aeternitatis* and to englobe the successiveness of men in the simultaneity of God."[5] But John seems not to have many followers. The successiveness of men is not objected to. *Post mortem* existence does not conflict with standards of myth widely acceptable to-day and not requiring substitution. Any discussion of immortality must emphasize that in every form it is a conception subject to the common human category of sense of time.

This unquestioned acceptability in many quarters is all the more striking since pre-existence — projecting from man's visible existence in the other direction — is one of the things that some of our demythologizing friends have ruled out. For the same reason they must be willing to exclude a *post mortem* existence both for Jesus and at the last day for those who believe in him. If they find currently unacceptable the view held by more than one New Testament writer that before Jesus' birth or incarnation he had enjoyed a noteworthy existence comparable to his later exaltation the latter must be rejected also. The two belong together. Interestingly enough, Wordsworth accepted as an intimation of future immortality precisely what he called "intimations" of pre-natal existence.

Actually contemporary theologians — and I name no names — are not agreed as to where the demythologizing should begin and end. The imaginative spheres to which the expression of religious experience are transposed include several — chronology, theology,

---

[4] See the excellent paper, "The Biblical View of Time", by James Muilenburg in *Harvard Theological Review*, LIV (1961), pp. 228-52.

[5] *Encyclopedia Britannica*, s.v. "John, Gospel of St".

and anthropology, as well as cosmology. Which of these categories may we retain in the primitive New Testament form, and which must be demythologized? Unconsciously we tend to retain part and revise part. Each person wishes to salvage what seems meaningful to himself. To others the full biblical *Weltanschauung* appears to be a kind of seamless robe to be either accepted or rejected in its entirety.

The need for demythologizing the futurist hope of the first Christians was evidently felt, if not expressed, in an early period of Christian history. For ultimately and in some respects quite soon much of it was translated to other forms of expression; if one may use the word, it was remythologized. Something like the Greek Platonic view of immortality unconsciously modified the expression of normative Jewish resurrection beliefs. We suspect this already in Paul, as we are reasonably sure of it in Josephus' description of Pharisaism. But as often happens, the old and new continued side by side in uneasy juxtaposition, and without the thorough supremacy of either view. The gradual increase of the immortality concept can no doubt be traced, and its reasons understood. The parallel persistence of the doctrine of bodily resurrection, not merely because of the authority of the New Testament and the Creeds but also because of human nature's craving for the familiar assurance of sensory phenomena, is also intelligible.

There are both advantages and disadvantages in focusing our inquiry upon the teachings of Jesus. The advantages are these: Whatever he thought or felt about the future during his ministry is little likely to have been influenced by his own later resurrection. For his followers, as we have already noted, this event, accepted as a past fact of experience, had a great influence when they looked backward or when they looked forward to the more general resurrection in the future. Our Synoptic Gospels record sayings of Jesus anticipating that he would not only be killed, but also would "rise after three days".[6] But the genuineness of the sayings may be doubted, or in any case the effect of the actual event is not likely to have acted in advance on the mind of Jesus or the minds of those

---

[6] Mark 8. 31; 9. 31; 10. 34. The parallels say "on the third day", and, in Matthew, "be raised". In general, resurrection is expressed in the New Testament as "from the dead" (ἐκ νεκρῶν) not "of the dead."

who heard him. Only afterwards did the individual event that was past play a part in visualizing and confirming the collective event that was future, as indeed it affected nearly every phase of Christian thinking.

Before his death Jesus and his disciples were spared the problem that has bothered men ever since, even down to the recent publication of a teacher in this school,[7] the relation of a resurrection conceived as an historical event to future theological belief. Epistemology seems to ask more difficult questions about actual events than about merely anticipated events.

Furthermore Jesus, unlike us moderns though not unlike his early followers, found little difficulty with the miracle involved in resurrection from the dead. That it was or would be supernatural rather than natural, if one may use a distinction scarcely known to him, he very likely took for granted. Several stories of individuals raised from the dead by Jesus or Peter or Paul are reported by the Synoptic writers much as are the stories of miraculous cure of the sick. For the whole of the New Testament we may be sure that the all-penetrating theism of the outlook on nature and history, left unraised the question whether resurrection from the dead was an automatic process inherent in the constitution of man, as in some other cultures the continuance of immortal souls is felt to be. On the contrary it was believed that only God could give power to raise the dead, and Jesus and his contemporaries, even in their more critical moods, were little concerned to question the possibility of what God had done and would do.

Finally Jesus' views of after-life are unlikely to have been affected by what we call the Greek conception. Some Jews of that general period, through contact with things unsemitic, may have been influenced by the doctrine of immortality. It is more likely to be found in the Apocrypha of the Old Testament and in Jewish apocalypses than in the Hebrew or rabbinic writings. I think Greek influence on Ecclesiastes has not been made out.

What concerns us here is the probability that Jesus himself was less likely to conflate with Jewish conceptions of resurrection alien parallels than were Paul, the authors of Hebrews and of John, and even than the authors of Luke-Acts and of the other Synoptic

---

[7] R. R. Niebuhr, *Resurrection and Historical Reason*, 1957.

Gospels. How alien, not to say mutually exclusive, the two concepts are to each other was brought to our attention by Professor Cullmann in his recent Ingersoll Lecture. And it is well to remind ourselves of the clear-cut words of Justin Martyr in his *Dialogue with Trypho,* lxxx, written after a full century of Christianity:

> If you have met with some so-called Christians who do not accept this (resurrection and millenium) but dare to blaspheme the God of Abraham, the God of Isaac, and the God of Jacob, who affirm that there is no resurrection of the dead but that when they die their souls are taken up to heaven, do not suppose that they are Christians. . . . But I and any Christians who are orthodox on all points know that there will be a resurrection of the flesh, etc.

The disadvantages of focusing our attention upon Jesus' view of the after-life are also obvious. His thought must if possible be discovered behind the reported sayings in the Gospels, especially the first three of them. This is a familiar difficulty whenever one seeks to get at his mind on any subject. But it is not only the ultimate evangelist that has to be allowed for. Between him and Jesus, oral if not written tradition has been at work, altering and varying the original viewpoint. This accounts for most of the apparent discrepancies among the Synoptic sayings of Jesus, since the single units of tradition had passed through different media in the process. Even the original expressions of Jesus might well have seemed to us obscure or contradictory, as do those of Paul from whom we have first-hand records in his genuine letters. In the case of Jesus unresolved variations of viewpoint about the after life are fully as apparent.

Beside all this we shall find the amount of relevant material quite scanty. No matter how abundant Jesus' references to the future appear to be—and none of the devices of scholarship has yet succeeded in reducing the extent to which we have come to recognize the futuristic element in the teaching of Jesus—on certain aspects of that future Jesus has in our records less to say than might have been expected. The resurrection as distinct from the judgement is not often separately described, nor is the nature of life after the judgement. As in many other Christian sources much less is said of the fate of the condemned than of the blessed, and much less about individuals than about groups.

This paucity of clear exposition is intelligible if we are right in thinking that, whatever our temporary focus now may be, it was not a major concern of Jesus to expound or reassert the views of the future life which he held or shared. His references to it are mainly incidental, and associated in a subordinate way with his major interests. This is increasingly clear of the whole complex of ideas which we call eschatology, to which our present subject belongs. Even the Kingdom of God for all its frequency of mention in our records is not the central concern of the Gospels. The same may be said of the resurrection or "eternal life". Their mention is nearly always incidental to something else.

Perhaps this is most readily illustrated in the Beatitudes, where we have in each sentence first a selected quality or condition for which men are to be congratulated and then in the second line of each couplet a variety of expressions of reward—"Theirs is the Kingdom of Heaven" (twice), "They shall see God", "They shall be called sons of God", "Your reward is great in heaven". Not all the references are *post mortem*, though some plainly are, and others are ambiguous or indecisive in their implications of time. In so far as they are *post mortem* they refer to reward or punishment, to advantage or disadvantage, to gain or loss. They are parallel to incidental references about more immediate results to the living.

On the resurrection itself Jesus once is represented as being drawn out in debate. The passage occurs in Mark and is reproduced in Matthew and Luke in evident dependence upon Mark (Mark 12. 18-27; Matt. 22. 23-33; Luke 20. 27-38). The passage belongs to the category and to the series of test questions. Sadducees, who as a group deny the resurrection, are the questioners and frame a question intended to reduce the idea to absurdity by instancing one woman who by Levirate law for childless widows had been married in turn to seven brothers. The question is asked, Whose wife will she be in the resurrection? (Incidentally this is perhaps the first place in the Bible where monogamy is most definitely assumed.)

Jesus' reply plainly accepts and argues for the doctrine of the resurrection. It disposes of the supposed assumption of plural marriage by declaring that when they rise from the dead they neither marry nor are given in marriage but are like angels in heaven. (Again it may seem odd that the clearest descriptive datum of the future life in the Gospels is the absence of marriage; —a view which some of the rabbis shared though others denied.) In the reply Jesus also meets not the specific instance but the scepticism about the resurrection belief by declaring that his questioners are wrong because they "know neither the scriptures nor the power of God". These are both of them points made by the rabbis in debate. God's power to raise the dead, they claim, is no greater than his power to create men by birth—an *a fortiori* argument that must be accepted. This is not explicitly included in the Gospel passage. But it does include a typical argument from scripture:

> But as for the dead being raised, have you not read in the book of Moses, in the passage about the Bush, how God said to him, "I am the God of Abraham, the God of Isaac, the God of Jacob?" He is not God of the dead but of the living. You are quite wrong.

The argument here is characteristically Jewish.[8] The rabbis, and I think other Jews and Christians, deduced contemporaneity of Moses with the patriarchs from pronouns and tenses and other grammatical phenomena in the texts of scripture. What God said to Moses involves survival or revival for Abraham, Isaac, and Jacob. It is because they anticipated this future that according to Heb. 11. 16, "God is not ashamed to be called their God". Similarly according to John 8. 56 Abraham had seen the day of Christ.

This single synoptic passage is in its general tenor self-evidently Jewish. It clearly puts Jesus on the side of the belief in resurrection along with the Pharisees, the rabbis, and presumably the weight of official Judaism going back as far as the second benediction in the daily prayer of Eighteen (*Shemoneh 'Esreh*). I see no reason why this Jewishness, or this concern for a theological question unusual in these Gospels (but compare the discussion of the Messiah's sonship in the very next section), should lead us to doubt the correctness of its ascription to Jesus of an acceptance of current ideas. At least he was no Sadducee. Luke, who makes some changes in the words of Jesus here, does not pass beyond the range of current Jewish speculation.

The other and minor references to the subject of future life do

---

[8] See my *Peril of Modernizing Jesus*, 1937 (reprinted 1962), pp. 59 f., 61-3, with notes.

not match this one synoptic passage in directness or explicitness. They are, as has been said, incidental. Only once again is any general resurrection mentioned, though it is described as the resurrection of the righteous. At Luke 14. 14, in a passage comparing the result of dinner invitations extended respectively to one's associates or equals and to the underprivileged, Jesus explains that the first will return the invitation while the others cannot, but "you will be repaid at the resurrection of the just". The reference here to the righteous only cannot be pressed, since the same evangelist elsewhere writes that "there will be a resurrection of both the righteous and the unrighteous" (Acts 24. 15).

There is also in Luke (16. 19-31) the parable of the rich man and Lazarus where, as in some of the Beatitudes, and especially in the woes and beatitudes of Luke, compensation is conspicuous rather by way of reversal or equalization than as reward and punishment. As Abraham said to the rich man, "Son, remember that you in your lifetime received your good things and Lazarus in like manner evil things; but now he is comforted here and you are in anguish."

This parable is noteworthy in other respects; the situation is pictured prior to any resurrection. Both of the deceased have been transported promptly to Hades, where they occupy two compartments separated by "a great gulf" but not preventing intercommunication. One is pleasant, the bosom of Abraham, the other a place of torment with the anguish of flame.

It is worthwhile to pause here to remind ourselves how often Abraham or all three of the patriarchs represent in Christian documents the charter members, or the hosts, or the primary examples of the resurrection experience. Beside this reference to Abraham as presiding over the situation between Dives and Lazarus, we have already mentioned the answer of Jesus to the Sadducees in Mark 12 and parallels and the passages in John 8 and in Hebrews 11 and from a later period the statement of Justin Martyr that to deny the resurrection is to blaspheme the God of Abraham, the God of Isaac, and the God of Jacob. There is also the earlier saying, Matt. 8. 11 (cf. Luke 13. 28, from Q ?), which anticipates the same three as the nucleus of membership in the Kingdom of God: "I tell you, many will come from east and west and will recline at table with Abraham, Isaac, and Jacob in the kingdom of heaven."

Perhaps the same reason underlies the mention of the same three in Acts 3. 13 in a context referring ("glorified"; "raised from the dead") to the resurrection of Jesus. Assurance in the resurrection of the patriarchs, though differently arrived at from the assurance in the resurrection of Jesus, seems to have served in Judaism and Jewish Christianity the same purpose as "first fruits" which that of Jesus did later.

The concept of reward or punishment undeferred at death recurs also in another Lucan passage where Jesus on the cross says to the penitent thief, "To-day you will be with me in Paradise" (Luke 23. 43).

This is not the place for the collection and minute examination of all synoptic passages relevant to our topic. That has been done by others and it leaves a confused and contradictory impression. Not even when the words of Jesus are compared with the more abundant Jewish materials and are found to coincide with them, whether from the apocalypses, from the Hellenistic writings, or from Talmud and Midrash, is the situation much better. Evidently the several sources exercised much freedom in imagining the subject, in recasting and varying the imagery. Even matters of place and time, or places and times, in the *post mortem* experience of the dead were not consistently plotted and mapped. The reasons can be easily guessed—the inherent unreality of the subject, the consequent conjecture and inference based on the equally fragmentary and unprecise statements in scripture, and the fusion of ideals of collective or national destiny with the problems of individual fate. There is inevitable vacillation between what is conceived as happening to the individual at once after death, and what occurs simultaneously to all men at the time of the final judgement. Approximate differentiation of good and evil men seems desirable both at once and ultimately. Hence one gets in other sources such implications or combinations as a first and a second death, a first and second resurrection, the days of the Messiah and the Kingdom of God. Whether the scene of these events is the earth as we know it or as it will be transformed, or elsewhere—Hades, Gehenna, heaven, paradise, or "the eternal habitations" (Luke 16. 9)—is equally ambiguous.

Even if we had more words of Jesus on the subject and if we were sure they were all correctly reported, one may doubt whether they would add up to a blueprint that would carry even for the devout believer a satisfying and authoritative picture as of a principal concern of Jesus' teaching. The very incidental character of the references suggests alike two almost contradictory conclusions.

1. The after-life was taken for granted by Jesus and by his hearers generally. He did not need to impress it or correct it. It was not for him or them a question of hesitation and debate. It is therefore an assured ingredient of his perspective.

2. By the same token his allusions do not allow us to reconstruct any very definite or circumstantial impression of this future. They were innocently unprecise, intimations rather than descriptions, and were employed in connection with other matters on which Jesus had something emphatic and significant to say.

In other words, the more sure we are that Jesus in fact accepted the perspective of those who believe in future existence, the more evident it seems that it was not the centre of his interest but was thought of and felt as relevant to questions of here and now. For him and for us it was part of the morrow about which neither he nor we need be anxious. If death of the body is not to be feared, if one is to go one's way to-day and to-morrow whatever the third day has in store, there is no need for the comforting thoughts of an after-life to banish the fear of death. We have lately had from the pen of John Knox a very honest inquiry into the problem of knowing what Jesus' death meant in anticipation to Jesus himself.[9] It will be more difficult to answer a like question about his personal and private employment of any anticipation of survival or revival. Our oldest records report primarily what was extrovert about him, and I think we must confine ourselves to this aspect of our records if we are to escape the extremes of fanciful imagination.

We cannot assume that the ideas and motives that had marked the origin of the resurrection faith in late Judaism always remained emphatic nor that the meanings that later Christians have found in it were already in the thought of Jesus. Clearly certain English words into which his sayings have been translated have come to have for us connotations that were not in their originals. "Eternal" (αἰώνιος) lacked its emphasis upon endlessness, though not on futurity. "Heaven" lacked the modern suggestion of futurity

[9] John Knox, *The Death of Christ*, 1958, chapter 5.

though not of otherworldliness. With one possible exception [10] neither "soul" nor "spirit" is used in the futuristic sense. Just as Jews and Christians have read into Old Testament passages a belief in resurrection that was not there, so more recent Christians have read into New Testament passages a belief in immortality instead of resurrection.

The religious and philosophical values of a future life to Jesus were perhaps less self-centred than they were later. There was an altruistic element in the anxiety of the living about the dead, as we understand the passages already cited from Daniel and 1 Thessalonians. The living needed assurance that the deserving dead would not miss the good things that the righteous living expected, and (in Daniel) that the wicked who had died would not escape the penalty that was their due. Resurrection as distinct from immortality is not the avoidance of death but revival after death. The length of interval between death and revival is not indicated. If Jesus sometimes emphasizes the nearness of the Kingdom he is shortening the interval not so much for the dead as for the many living who would "not taste of death". Obviously this differs a good deal from any modern concern for the situation *after death*.

There is no evidence that for Jesus the after-life was regarded as showing that values in this life are durable and therefore precious. Nor on the other hand is it an expression of the opposite of this life with the latter's mutability. It spells neither continuity nor discontinuity, neither unity nor the kind of duality which is so natural in our tendency to contrast the material and the spiritual, the secular and the sacred. Such philosophical approaches are not typical of Jesus.

To-day it is a satisfying belief that the future life will have social attractions—the company of those whom we have loved and unimpeded fellowship with God. This ideal is not explicit in the limited gospel material and probably not implicit. There is more if not better company in the wide road that leads to destruction than in the narrow one leading to life. To meet modern tastes one would have to spiritualize such descriptions as we have of dining in the Kingdom of God and to deliteralize the fire in Gehenna and gnashing of teeth in the outer darkness. If Jesus tells the penitent

---

[10] Matt. 10. 28. Cf. H. B. Sharman, *The Teaching of Jesus about the Future*, 1909, pp. 267-70.

thief, "To-day you will be with me in Paradise," the accent is on the place or time not the company.

References to the future life for Jesus as for Judaism in general are connected with the idea of retribution. It may not be clear whether that life itself is retributive to the good alone, or whether resurrection is prior to a judgement at which rewards and penalties are allotted, or mainly a subsequent period in which they are carried out. Whatever the extent or the sequence visualized concerning resurrection, judgement, and ultimate *post mortem* experience, these are part of an inseparable group of ideas and have to do with the consequences of our behaviour here. Formally at least the future is the sanction for what is recommended now. In so far as that future is after death, or without death at the *parousia*, or even in the normal nearer sequels in this age—and often the sayings of Jesus put these parallel, or leave them undistinguished —the recommendations are intended to warn or promise. This utilitarian-sounding approach would suit the standpoint of his hearers. Jesus' own difference of emphasis would lie in what he recommends, not on why he recommends it. Even sacrificial, disinterested conduct is rarely mentioned by him without appeal to future consequence.

This appeal to the future may have been conventional. Jesus does not seem concerned to give instruction about the future for its own sake. Recommendations on conduct here and now were his main concern. Since he felt these to be valid, self-evident— or in religious language, the will of God—he was sure they deserved and would receive, sooner or later, due reward, and their opposites likewise the reverse. He may have emphasized the nearness of the end, shortness of the time, and the consequent urgency of right action. In so doing he was not revising the future programme, or making special claims for himself, but out of "pastoral" concern was underscoring the importance of the critical choices or changes which men have to make.[11]

Such is the context in which the scattered allusions to man's fate after death occur in the older Gospels. They do not suggest a high degree of otherworldliness. They are related and relevant to be-

[11] The ethical implications of such sanction are well discussed by A. N. Wilder, *Eschatology and Ethics in the Teaching of Jesus*, Revised Edition, 1950.

haviour in this life. They leave unanswered a whole host of modern questions about the biological and psychological nature of man, about death and consciousness, about personality. They give us little for a twentieth-century prospectus on the future—even for a tidy first-century eschatology.

More offensive than what they omit is what they imply. The synoptic intimations of a future existence are in the form of sanctions for recommended conduct. No matter how wise and true the ethical standards or the futuristic insights, their association is likely to seem a scandal. One merely cannot say which seems worse to a kind of present-day religion. Is it worse that goodness here and now should be recommended by regard for future reward and threat and that disinterested virtue should be associated with practical utilitarian considerations? Or is it worse that the spiritual ideal, which over the centuries has been refined and expressed in terms of the state of the blessed dead, should be debased by being traced back to the crude motivation in this life of escaping future punishment or gaining future rewards?

I understand that some have felt that a recent Ingersoll lecturer described the New Testament faith in the future as the wrong kind.[12] Thy will perhaps feel that to-day it is being attributed to "the wrong reason". Yet it is inevitable that this element should appear here as it does everywhere else in the Gospels. It has been described as "the perpetual twofold issue of all preaching of the gospel: the offer of mercy and the threat of impending judgement inseparable from it, salvation and destruction, life and death".[13] This, if anything, is an authentic feature of Jesus' teaching.

Can we go any further than this? Or shall we abandon Jesus' eschatology *in toto* as part of outgrown myth and start afresh from the framework of our modern thought, ethical, philosophical, and scientific, to construct our own hypothesis concerning a future life?

The paucity and incidental character of Jesus' references can be interpreted as justifying such treatment. It has been suggested

---

[12] O. Cullmann, "Immortality of the Soul and Resurrection of the Dead: The Witness of the New Testament," *Harvard Divinity School Annual Lectures and Book Reviews*, No. 21, 1955-6; published also in French, and separately in 1958 in English (London: Epworth Press; New York: The Macmillan Co.).

[13] J. Jeremias, *The Parables of Jesus*, Eng. Trans., 1954, pp. 15 f.

that Jesus usually and deliberately was silent on these themes.[14] The answer to the Sadducees may show him impatient of the crudity of the view of the after-life without attempting to substitute a more spiritual view. There is a specially striking conclusion —"punch line", in the vernacular—of the story of Dives and Lazarus. When the rich man wishes his surviving brothers warned of the torment of the damned by a messenger actually sent from Hades, he receives the answer, "If they do not hear Moses and the prophets neither will they be convinced if some one should rise from the dead." Twice Dives urges that such a messenger could successfully warn them so that they would repent. Twice Abraham indicates that resurrection has no convincing evidential value, when compared with scriptural warning already available. According to this word, so surprising for any early Christian document, reformed conduct in this life would not be promoted by more convincing evidence of the future life or judgement. What Jesus omits to emphasize in his teaching about the future is no great loss. It would add no useful influence.

Of course we can attempt to find behind his life and teaching presuppositions which at least for us would be logical and valid, though they too may be conventional in his environment. There is the belief in God, who has a will, and that will is man's duty. Those who disobey and those who obey will be treated according to their works. But beside this divine *lex talionis* there are two rather different principles at work. One is the idea that independently of individual merit God in the end equalizes good and bad experience for all men, so that evil now will be balanced with good hereafter and vice versa. This lies behind two passages in Luke. The other is the prophetic emphasis on God's sheer generosity, meting out to men more mercy than they deserve, a kind of divine example of "the second mile". In the theistic framework of Jesus and his contemporaries such theology and theodicy is to be expected.

Another indirect way of adding to the actual data of the Gospels is to make logical deductions of our own about a future life from

[14] It is noteworthy how often students of this field while admitting that Jesus shared the usual views on resurrection and general eschatology have concluded that "he felt very little interest in them". So, for example, W. G. Kümmel, *Promise and Fulfilment*, Eng. Trans., 1957, p. 92. Cf. the older statements, as in B. H. Streeter, *Immortality*, 1917, pp. 122 f.

other features of their story. We can believe that Jesus' ethical teaching shows what we should call the conservation of values, the sacredness of individual personality. There are passages where Jesus seems to predate into this life the eschatology of the future, and not merely to make this life determinative for that future. Thus continuity does occur, but in the reverse direction. Scholars are not agreed as to how far proleptic or "realized" eschatology is implied in Jesus' words. From the early days of the Church some have understood that foretastes or intimations of the life to come were to be found in the character and historic career of Jesus, and then and now in the life here on earth of his followers. The more it is possible to expect and recognize in the present the ideal aspects of the life of the future, the less important does the prospect of later immortality become. Perfectionism as a present philosophy has usually diverted attention from the future, while emphasis upon moral and spiritual limitations of mankind and ourselves here and now have kindled that hope by sheer contrast. Men will differ as to how far the teaching of Jesus aligns itself with the sturdy expectation that men can and will hear and obey his words, and by obedience in this life will approximate his standards and will merit the future rewards. If Christianity has added little of value to the world's conception of a future life, it has rather offered a partial equivalent in our life here.

The Wordsworthian phrase "intimations of immortality" is not only a polysyllabic tongue-twister, but also each word is too easily confused, the first with "imitations", as in one edition of Dowden's introduction to the poet's works, the second with "immorality". The phrase is further only partly appropriate for the thought of Jesus. For him the alternatives were continuous living here until the *parousia* and into whatever is in store for men thereafter, or else death followed after an interval of unspecified length and character by a general and/or individual experience of being raised from among the dead. In no strict sense is either of these what we usually mean by immortality.

On the other hand, "intimation" is not a bad description of the nature of the Gospel material. According to the dictionary the word means hint, indirect or obscure allusion, or suggestion. This is precisely what the Gospels do give us.

What is more, they indicate the context of the references. They are not speculative but practical. They are associated with Jesus' conversations on conduct. To Jesus and his Jewish contemporaries under the Law the urgent problem was not what to believe but what to do. This was the predicament of man to which he addressed himself. He was for his day and outlook a true existentialist.

The outlook was, however, conditioned. Jesus believed in a God who worked miracles and rewarded righteousness. Any future life, like every present life, is the individual work of God. Man as man is not inherently immortal, nor indeed is any part of him. His body and soul both come into being and they both can go out of being and can both come back into being.

Overshadowing any interest in what would befall his hearers if they should die before the *parousia*, and what would happen or had happened to many generations of men who had died, was the expectation of what would overtake the living. At least that appears to be the perspective of Jesus in the Synoptic Gospels. In John's Gospel this is not so clearly the case. Instead of the many who will not taste of death, we have there Lazarus of Bethany who at least did die and was brought back to life, and only the possibility that one unnamed disciple, unlike Peter, might perhaps tarry until the Lord comes.

The expectation of living on until the *parousia* may be the real reason why the Gospels say so little of resurrection. It excludes also the usual idea of immortality as following death. In other words, one may say that eschatology of this sort replaces the need for much concern in the subjects appropriate to this lecture, when defined as after death.

I am no expert on the Qumran texts but I do know that they too are heavily surcharged with vivid eschatological pictures, and yet so far as I can tell the published documents have little or no clear reference either to immortality or to resurrection from the dead. It ought not to be attributed to the texts just because Josephus includes in Essene eschatology the immortality of the soul as he does in Pharisaic belief, and Hippolytus attributes to the Essenes' faith also resurrection of the body.[15] Perhaps the Qumran documents illustrate how attention when concentrated on apocalyptic hope may leave out as relatively unimportant the question what happens to those who *do* die. I have assumed that the subject of this lecture calls for the latter question. Perhaps I am wrong. In that case immortality should have been construed as including the whole synoptic eschatology and should not have been limited to such passages as imply actual death. The line is confessedly not always clear. But except to modern millenarians the answer of Jesus about those who taste of death would be of more interest than about those who literally will never die. Certainly the first would be at most an intimation of the second.

© Copyright 1960 by the President and Fellows of Harvard College.

[15] The material is of course extensive. I refer only to two essays. For the literary sources on the Essenes see Morton Smith, *Hebrew Union College Annual*, xxix, 1958, pp. 273-313; for the absence thus far of convincing evidence of resurrection belief from Qumran see the unpublished thesis of George Wesley Buchanan, Drew University, 1959, "The Eschatological Expectations of the Qumran Community", chapter 5, note 4.

www.ingramcontent.com/pod-product-compliance
Lightning Source LLC
Chambersburg PA
CBHW070932160426
43193CB00011B/1668